JESSE FINK

15 DAYS IN JUNE

HOW AUSTRALIA BECAME A FOOTBALL NATION

untapped

ABOUT *UNTAPPED*

Most Australian books ever written have fallen out of print and become unavailable for purchase or loan from libraries. This includes important local and national histories, biographies and memoirs, beloved children's titles, and even winners of glittering literary prizes such as the Miles Franklin Literary Award.

Supported by funding from state and territory libraries, philanthropists and the Australian Research Council, *Untapped* is identifying Australia's culturally important lost books, digitising them, and promoting them to new generations of readers. As well as providing access to lost books and a new source of revenue for their writers, the *Untapped* collaboration is supporting new research into the economic value of authors' reversion rights and book promotion by libraries, and the relationship between library lending and digital book sales. The results will feed into public policy discussions about how we can better support Australian authors, readers and culture.

See untapped.org.au for more information, including a full list of project partners and rediscovered books.

Readers are reminded that these books are products of their time. Some may contain language or reflect views that might now be found offensive or inappropriate.

For Pim Verbeek (RIP). I miss you, my friend

CONTENTS

FOREWORD
BY GEORGE NEGUS

Why the fuss? Why the fervour sweeping the land? Why has Australia suddenly transformed into a nation of 20 million 'real' football fans?

Why the wild euphoria and proud national afterglow? Why the rapturous talkback radio or the blanket commercial television air time, the saturation print coverage or the front-page banner headlines or the colour liftouts or the endless column inches telling us everything about our national football team from Mark Schwarzer's favourite food to the names of Harry Kewell's kids?

Why the dramatic change of heart? Why are we all suddenly right behind the Socceroos, on 'the bandwagon'?

The period documented in this book, from our qualification for the 2006 World Cup to our debut at the 2007 Asian Cup, has been like no other in the history of Australian football. Millions of Australians, millions no one knew existed, have turned out to be closet football fans. And to think we lifelong diehards felt we were walking alone!

The reason for all this profound change is simple: it finally dawned on this pathologically sport-mad land that football's quadrennial World Cup really is The Big One. Not the Bulldogs vs the Broncos, West Coast vs the Swans, Lil' Lleyton vs the Swiss, not even Australia vs the Poms in cricket or the Kiwis in rugby.

The fact is, as Jesse Fink so eloquently reveals throughout what you are about to enjoy, the 'world game' is not just a sport, not just a game, not just a weekend pastime—but an earthly religion, a way of being, an expression of identity.

For pathetic football nuts like Jesse and me—badge-wearing

members of the so-called Australian 'football family'—the Socceroos making it to Germany was close to therapy, certainly a hell of a lot cheaper than the sessions we would have needed with a shrink had they not qualified. Being drowned in beer in the famous Hofbräuhaus in Munich before the game against Brazil was like a combination cleansing of past Socceroos sins and a World Cup baptism. We had joined a different kind of League of Nations, the football 'league of nations', something we feared we'd never see in our lifetimes.

For most of the other close to 200 countries in the world, football is part of their collective psyche, what they believe themselves to be. As the legendary Liverpool coach Bill Shankly put it: Football is not a matter of life and death—it is far more important.

I've always felt that, deep down, Australians knew this; that it was just a matter of time before football's extraordinary impact politically, economically and culturally on the rest of the world would be felt here. Perhaps that day has come.

If it has, there are no more apt ambassadors for Australia than the Socceroos. They are a thumbprint of our nation at a time when the misguided xenophobes among us are questioning multiculturalism. Take a look at the names on those green-and-gold jerseys that Australians from six to 60 are now banging down store doors to buy and pull on like their new heroes: Schwarzer, Neill, Kisnorbo, Thwaite, Chipperfield, Grella, Bresciano, Culina, Cahill, Emerton, Sterjovski, Kewell, Skoko, Aloisi, Kennedy, Holman, Viduka, Steffanuto, Valeri, Carle.

Whether the Socceroos and Australian football can maintain their newfound momentum is both debatable and problematic. Whoever succeeds Dutch magician Guus Hiddink as our next World Cup coach has gigantic football boots to fill. Can the next wave of Socceroos lift themselves onto the world's most demanding sporting stage the way Viduka's men did?

And do we really have what it takes to meet the challenge of the tricky Asian adventure? As a trading nation, we've struggled to make it with and against the Asians, so what about our mettle as a football nation? We are, after all, still in football's third world, a *developing,* not a developed, nation. Asia will test our regional clout. Our welcome into the Asian Football Confederation has been mixed and qualified and the ambitious Asians will no doubt enjoy cutting us back to our previous size. 'Don't get cocky' will be their message on and off the pitch.

Right now, though, post-World Cup 2006 and with the Asian Cup imminent, the battle of the codes in this country is well and truly on. 'The sleeping giant' of Australian sport has been roused.

Jesse Fink, a personal and professional mate with both his heart and mind in Australian football, has definitely captured those magical '15 days in June', when Australia woke up and realised it was a football nation.

PREFACE

'When Australia qualifies for the next World Cup, this country is going to go berserk.'

JOHNNY WARREN, 2003

At quarter to midnight on 16 November 2005, I was standing in the media box at Telstra Stadium in Sydney, wedged between a stunned Japanese FIFA official and an Italian bloke who'd sneaked his way into the enclosure by borrowing a pass from a friend. The Italian had tears streaming down his face. Both men couldn't believe what they'd just seen. I had to take their word for it. Like many of the 83,000 at the stadium, and the eight million watching around the country, I hadn't been able to bring myself to look. In truth, I'd buried my face in the armpit of the Italian bloke's leather jacket. He didn't seem to mind. 'I understand, mate, it's alright,' he laughed, when I apologised afterwards.

The noise inside the ground was so loud and unearthly it was as if I'd pressed my ear up against the jet engine of an airplane. The stands rippled with movement and colour, like fields of blooming canola. I could vaguely make out what looked like Australia's Spain-based striker John Aloisi running down the far sideline with ten maniacs in full playing kit chasing him, bench players and team officials in their wake. I turned around to the radio booth behind me to see ABC commentators Peter Wilkins and Andy Harper thumping the perspex window with their fists and almost expiring from excitement. High fives were flying everywhere. Grown men were hugging and kissing. The flute solo in Men at Work's 'Down Under' filled the late spring air, along with fireworks, yellow streamers and all manner of rubbish. 'We've done it!' said the Italian bloke, clasping my wrist. 'I don't fucking believe it. We've done it!' He wiped the tears from his eyes with the sleeve of his jacket.

We'd done it. We'd finally made it to the FIFA World Cup, the biggest sporting event on earth, after 32 excruciating years. Nineteen seventy-four was a long time ago. It was another *time*. Patty Hearst. Richard Nixon. Cyclone Tracy. Now it had all come full circle, but what the hell had happened? What sort of perverse logic was at work here? This had been one of the worst prepared qualifying campaigns in living memory. The new coach, a Dutch gun-for-hire called Guus Hiddink, who'd almost torn his hair out watching his 'boys' scrape to a 2-1 qualifying win over the Solomon Islands in a Honiara cow paddock, had said we'd need a 'miracle' to make it through. He'd only been five weeks in the job and had engineered victory over a team that hadn't lost a game in South America in the second half of its qualifying campaign, even against world-beaters Brazil and Argentina. Now we were going to Deutschland 2006. The jinx was over. The hoodoo shattered.

As first a fan, then a sports journalist obsessed with this team of no-hopers, I had spent some of the best years of my life dreaming of this very day. I'd lived through the agony of Argentina in 1993, Iran in 1997, Uruguay in 2001. I could remember where I was for each of them, when that first hit to the guts came, why I persisted in believing in the Socceroos when it would have been easier to just give up and walk away. But now that it had come, I didn't know what to think, having been so habitually conditioned to watching them lose. I sat back down in my seat and gathered my thoughts. So Australia had qualified—what were we supposed to do now?

Set aside June 2006, for starters. The next morning I went to my local bookstore to get some literary inspiration for the trip I planned to make to Germany. I walked over to the travel section, gave the racks a quick once-over and came up with ...

nothing. *Nichts.* While I had the choice of more than 500 books about growing olives in Italy or buying condemned buildings from canny geriatrics in France, if I wanted anything about Germany, the kindly shop assistant told me, I'd be better off looking in History or Military Studies. That wasn't what I wanted. So I tried the local library. The same. No *A Year in Morgenröthe-Rautenkratz* or *Under the Thuringian Sun* on any shelves, anywhere. Publishers clearly didn't see much of a market for books about vacationing in a land that had given rise to Martin Luther, Adolf Hitler and Boney M. Aside from guidebooks, there were no German travel books at all.

For most of us, Germany happily functions as the setting for a midday war movie or as a subject we took in high school. We can all reference it by important points in its history or popular culture: Versailles; the Weimar Republic; the Holocaust; Dresden; JFK speaking at the opening of the Berlin Wall; David Hasselhoff torturing modern song at its fall; Alan Rickman's mincing performance as a sinister West German terrorist in the first *Die Hard;* that Kraftwerk album we bought on a whim and quickly tried to return. Yet beyond the parameters of murder, conflict, espionage and bad 1980s rock, Germany has scant meaningful presence in our daily lives.

We all own German products. We drink German beer. Some of us drive German cars. But to want to travel to a country, and to fully immerse oneself in its very essence, it must have more going for it than its GDP. Germany, unfortunately, possesses very little such appeal. Its most significant problem is not its Nazi heritage or the legacy of the Cold War, but simply that there are better places in Europe to visit. Like architecture and culture? Try Italy or France. Like good food and hot bodies? Go to Spain. Like sunshine and beaches? Book a ticket to Portugal or Croatia.

Although Germany remains the dominant economy in Europe, five million unemployed, the lowest birth rate in the EU and nearly zero per cent growth are proving problematic for a nation that has lived on the fruits of the *Wirtschaftswunder,* the so-called 'economic miracle'. This *Wirtschaftswunder,* the period between the end of the war and the fall of the wall, is fundamental to the identity of the German people. Germany's other 'miracle', the 'Miracle of Bern', when West Germany defeated Hungary in the final of the 1954 World Cup, is similarly crucial. When they had little to be proud of, sport offered them pride. In fact, Germany's relationship with sport is not unlike Australia's. We both feel validated by winning and like to vaunt our superiority. Little wonder, then, that from as early as 1992, Germany began planning a bid to host its third football World Cup.

Winning the right to host a World Cup is one thing. Winning the world over is another. So the German government decided to spend €3 million on a promotional campaign with the catchy slogan, '*Die Welt zu Gast bei Freunden*' or 'A Time to Make Friends'. It made no secret of the fact it was a tough assignment.

'We are known for our organisational talents and punctuality,' said Dr Christoph Bergner, German Interior Ministry state secretary. 'Unfortunately we are not viewed as especially friendly and therefore have a special challenge with the World Cup.'

German football giant Franz Beckenbauer, head of the German World Cup Organising Committee and a vice-president of FIFA, football's world governing body, announced at the press conference for the launch of the campaign in December 2005 that his country 'wouldn't get this opportunity again for another 50 years so it's worth at least smiling for a few weeks'. Straight from The Kaiser's mouth. Come to Germany, take note of all these happy smiley Germans, and spend your money, *bitte.*

I was one sceptic who didn't need convincing to return to Germany. I'd been there earlier in the year for *Inside Sport* magazine on a German government-sponsored junket, the highlight of which was seeing the Socceroos play in the FIFA Confederations Cup in Frankfurt, the traditional dry run for the World Cup. When the offer came, I didn't hesitate to accept. It was a chance to see our underplayed national team take on a powerhouse of the game, Germany, in a brand new arena that would host World Cup games. A once-in-a-lifetime opportunity to see Australia skipper Craig Moore lead his men onto the tartan pitch of the Waltstadion, amid the jeers of the boisterous and well-lubricated German fans, to line up opposite names like Ballack, Schweinsteiger, Podolski, Kahn—*proper* football names. My boss at *Inside Sport* was the fearsome Brad Boxall, a legendary figure in men's magazines who'd built his career on soft porn and rugby league. He didn't know Schweinsteiger from a bottle of Steinlager, but he graciously and unexpectedly took my word for it that the trip was worth it and agreed to let me go with a group of excited sports hacks for ten days.

It was a long way to go for one game, but the German government was keen to show our magazine's Australian readers that there was more to a World Cup than just football. Herded from hotel to hotel, city to city, we got to see with our own eyes what made Germany tick, who its people were, and how it was preparing to stage this massive event that, because the Socceroos always failed to qualify, still flew under the radar of most Australians. Over those ten days, my view of all things Teutonic began to change. The people were surprisingly friendly, the cities weren't that awful, the nightlife was as good as anywhere, if not better, and the country's horrendous past didn't seem as much of a burden on everyday German life as we had come to expect.

We got to see a mob of fans descend upon the white-haired Beckenbauer in his limousine outside the Waltstadion, as if he were a rock star. We witnessed the ridiculous pampering of FIFA officials at their hotel, carrying on like they were important heads of state. We had privileged access to explore the bowels of a World Cup stadium, AOL Arena, in the port city of Hamburg, and see the super-sized players' spas and the hangar-like garages that had been purpose-built to whisk in team buses so that players could avoid the melee of over-zealous fans outside. The scale of it all—the preparation that the World Cup demanded of its organisers—left us in suitable awe.

That's why, when Aloisi slotted home his penalty, I knew I had to go back. To start planning for a holiday I had never expected to take, like the tens of thousands of Australian football fans, both old diehards and new converts, making the very same plans. A lucky few would get match tickets. The majority would not, but would still come to Germany in their droves—good-humoured, passionate in their support and open to whatever fate rolled our way.

People like Christopher Stevenson from Albion Park, who was 20 metres underground when Australia defeated Uruguay. A miner at the Delta Colliery at Elouera, he didn't see any of the game live but when finally told about it at the end of his shift he was just as excited as if he'd been there. Now, on a jumbo bound for Frankfurt, he was on his way to the World Cup, with his adult son Daniel and brother-in-law Werner, an emigre from Germany. All three were resigned to not getting tickets, but they didn't seem to care. They were going for the hell of it and their better halves had given their blessings. 'We've got the best wives in the world,' said the mustachioed Werner.

One of Christopher's workmates, irony of ironies, was 1974 Socceroos captain Peter Wilson, who had famously turned his back on the game, shunned player reunions, and become a virtual recluse at his home in Kembla Heights, outside Wollongong. He'd refused to comment publicly on anything to do with the Socceroos, the 1974 version or any other. But when Christopher told Peter he was going to Germany, the old warrior's face lit up. 'Oh mate, you'll have a good time over there.'

I had a hunch that Australia's presence at the tournament would be a significant few weeks; not only because Australian football had finally found itself a global stage, but also because the rest of the world was given an opportunity to reassess its mostly hackneyed view of Australia. Some had already made the grandiose claim that our nation changed on the night of 16 November 2005, but that was premature. We won a football game to take one of the 32 spots at the World Cup. (If we had lost the tie—and we came very close to doing just that, save for a split-second's misjudgement from Alvaro Recoba in the 18th minute—football could easily have reverted to the dark ages.) The important moment for our country was still to come. That was in June, when we had at least three games to show the world we weren't a fluke, and that we deserved to be considered in the same company as Brazil, Argentina, Germany, France, Italy, Spain, Portugal and Holland.

Sport has always been vital to any reading of our national identity, but not before this World Cup had we the opportunity to compete, quite literally, against the rest of the planet in a sport that really counted for something. The whole world would be watching these three games—Chinese, Indians, Africans, Europeans, Americans, Japanese, Brazilians, Russians, Arabs, Melanesians, Israelis, Vietnamese, everybody. This was an opportunity our country had not had in over three decades. For 270 minutes, possibly more, we'd be able to show the world who we were, what we stood for, and how far we had come. Being in Germany was also an opportunity for self-evaluation. When we saw ourselves up close, would we like what we saw?

It was my fervent hope that with a great Australian side in Germany we would witness scenes much like those at Korea–Japan 2002 when Hiddink took the host nation to the semi-finals and triggered a wave of national pride no one had seen coming. The bedlam on the streets of the Korean capital, gridlocked with seven million screaming football converts in their 'Be the Reds!' T-shirts, was unprecedented.

Australia was obviously a different case to Korea in many ways. We weren't hosting a World Cup on home soil, nor, at that stage of our football development, had we the pedigree of the

Koreans. But there were enough similarities between the two countries for any comparison not to be trite. Both nations had long been encumbered with an inferiority complex: Australia for its convict past, Korea for its forced occupation by Japan in the early 20th century. Yet both were—and are—two of the most dynamic countries in their regions. Hiddink, the inscrutable, private Dutchman, had tapped into what made both countries tick, and made them believe that anything was possible.

He would inherit a very different team in Australia. Where the Koreans were defensively strong but bereft of attack, Australia was the opposite. Where Korean team culture was based on traditional hierarchical values, Australia's was intrinsically egalitarian. In the Socceroos, Hiddink found a team inculcated in a culture he could work with instantly. What he had to change was their skill level, organisational acumen and approach. Once those things had been sorted out, the rest would take care of itself. Theoretically.

As individuals, Hiddink's new 'project' might not have represented the best football talent in Europe, but as a unit they weren't about to collapse into a self-recriminating rabble when the going got tough, á la Portugal at Korea-Japan 2002. They would give their all, whatever odds were stacked against them. This was as much an opportunity for Hiddink to test his own adaptability as it was for Australia to win some football matches.

These were all the things I expected—or at least hoped—to see fulfilled in Germany. What I hadn't bargained on was returning home with a renewed appreciation of what already makes Australia great, World Cup success or not. Qualities all of us probably take for granted at one time or another but fiercely uphold by almost natural reflex. Though they would ultimately succumb in harsh circumstances to Italy in the second round, Hiddink's Socceroos showed even the biggest football powers that they could learn one or two things about how to play the game. For those 15 days in June, the world, briefly, turned on its axis.

Yet, amid the hype surrounding the Socceroos' achievement in Germany, it was the period that came *after* the national team's elimination that was arguably more important for the development of the Australian game. When Hiddink touched down in Moscow in late July, replacing Dynamo Moscow's Yuri Syomin as coach of Russia, a new chapter in Australia's football story began.

That narrative wasn't as easy to follow, and certainly wasn't as heroic, but would demonstrate just how much Australia had changed for its World Cup experience. Not all of what transpired was good. Some of it, in fact, saw Australian football get knocked down a few pegs—the announcement of John O'Neill's decision not to stay on as chief executive, the resignation of his prize recruit, Matt Carroll, as head of operations and the Kuwait City and Denmark meltdowns were all massive body blows to Football Federation Australia (FFA), an organisation that hadn't put a foot wrong in years. Two steps forward, one step back.

It's sobering to think that the Socceroos only won one game in Germany. Yet that one game changed our football and our country, both in the way we felt about ourselves and in the image Australia projected abroad.

When I began this book, I planned to write about Australia's adventure at the World Cup and some of the (mis)adventures that came afterwards, from the moment Australia defeated Uruguay in November 2005 through to the countdown to our first Asian Cup campaign in July 2007. Yet the more I analysed what took place during that period, the more I realised the full story had its roots deep in the game's mostly forgotten past, the dark epoch slagged off by the FFA marketing department as 'old soccer'.

15 Days in June isn't a definitive account of this period, nor have I slavishly hunted down every Australian player and official for their life stories—if readers are after the latter, they can't go wrong with Matthew Hall's *The Away Game,* which was recently adapted into a documentary. The history of the local code is also covered in Trevor Thompson's *One Fantastic Goal*, and the sport's grubby politics in Andrew Jennings's *Foul!* and Ross Solly's *Shoot Out*.

In truth, as any football journalist will tell you, not a lot of what players have to say is that interesting anyway. Sportsmen, like politicians, have been trained by their agents and minders to toe the team line, not to speak about personalities and to fudge answers when difficult questions are put to them. Thankfully, though, there are still some engaging characters inside and outside the Australian national team. Many of them were interviewed for this book. Those who chose not to take part were surprisingly few. One glaring omission was John O'Neill. Despite my issuing a year-long standing invitation, and repeated requests to his protective media minders, he declined to be involved. Whether it was because he feared criticism of his actions or ambitions or thought he was above scrutiny, I cannot say. In any case, his attitude to this project was perplexing. Perhaps the departing FFA chief executive was saving all the juicy stuff for his own inevitable autobiography.

In the end it scarcely mattered. What I found most fascinating about the Socceroos during my research was that they became a vehicle for a lot of the aspirations Australia had lost sight of during the Howard era—true 'engagement' with Asia, being open to new ideas, having a world vision. Football, as much as politics or economics, can change societies, something that has been proven at recent World Cups. The world game changed France, it changed Korea and Japan, it changed Germany. Remarkably, it's now changed Australia too. The Socceroos' 15 days at the FIFA World Cup in June 2006 represented a pivotal moment in our nationhood, The best part, though, is that even better days lie ahead.

Jesse Fink, Sydney, April 2007

FIRST HALF · WORLD CUP

CHAPTER ONE · WHAT WORLD CUP?

'I can't say it did anything for me because I'm not into the sport ... all they have done is qualify for a tournament.'

LEIGH MATTHEWS, 2005

Even now, a year and a half on from the time he made this comment, it beggars belief that such a pillar of Australian sport as Matthews, the great Hawthorn VFL rover and Brisbane AFL coach, could be so pig-headedly ignorant—or cynically dismissive—of what it means to qualify for a FIFA World Cup, the world's biggest sporting event. But in fairness to Matthews, the significance of the Socceroos' achievement on the morning of 17 November 2005 was lost not just on him but on a lot of people, though you wouldn't have guessed it from the public reaction.

Businesses near my home in Sydney's inner west had the front pages of the day's dailies sticky-taped to their windows. Green-and-gold streamers fluttered from the aerials of hotted-up cars. Commuters sipping their takeaway coffees were wearing green-and-gold 'AUSTRALIA' caps. In The Domain, a stretch of open parkland in the centre of the city, a stage was set up for the thousands of supporters—who had not had the opportunity or the inclination to sleep—to cheer their new heroes. *The Australian* published a photo of one fan, Steve Saunders, who had crawled out of his hospital bed and taken his drip with him. He was still recovering from a machete attack, of all things, but couldn't bear to stay away from the celebrations. 'It's a special day,' he told the paper. 'If anything, that's going to cure me.' His nurse had other ideas and escorted him back to the ward before the players emerged.

It was as if Australia's football tribes had suddenly found themselves in a parallel universe. How else to explain the tabloid *Daily Telegraph*'s front page the next day: 'THE HEROES 12-PAGE SOUVENIR LIFTOUT. THE NIGHT OUR ROOS LIVED THEIR DREAM'? *Our* Roos? This coming from a paper that would have reserved its dying breath to stick the knife into football? What was going on? SBS earned its highest ratings in a quarter of a century. The national broadcaster, the ABC, ran with the news of the Socceroos' win for the first six minutes of its 7 pm bulletin. No other single sporting event in memory had received such exposure. Even Legends Genuine Memorabilia, the heartbeat of sporting middle Australia, rushed a thousand copies of 'DESTINY FULFILLED', a 'superb panograph' comprising 'a montage of memorable imagery from that special night' into stores. All for $348, or $166 in three 'easy monthly payments'. Counterfeits, made from crude colour photocopies, flooded the market. My local cafe was selling them by the Friday.

The Socceroos' win was even held up by some federal politicians as a defining moment for multicultural Australia, a vindication of the immigration policies pursued by Liberal and Labor governments since the meat-and-two-veg days of Arthur Calwell and the White Australia Policy. This lofty claim, however, was undermined a few weeks later when mobs of Lebanese hoodlums and Anglo-Saxon 'skip' thugs laid into each other with fists, boots and beer bottles in Australia's biggest race riots since the 1850s. It was a reality check for anyone who felt the Socceroos had helped our country turn an important corner. Sometimes, winning a game of football can only do so much.

As those shameful events would attest, Australia had not changed per se, but the Socceroos had tapped into *something*. Post 16 November, our country felt like a different place, the victory over Uruguay evoking passions that had hitherto lain dormant. But when the draw for the finals was held and the

Aussies were bundled into a group with world champions Brazil, 1998 semi-finalists Croatia and reigning Asian champions Japan, the good cheer turned to cheerful resignation. Whatever it meant for our country going to a World Cup, Australia wasn't going to last very long at all.

The Socceroos' tournament was as good as over. Just turning up, the critics argued, was ample reward for a code that still had years of hard work to put in before it could capture Australians' hearts and souls. Aussie Rules, rugby league and cricket were unassailable. Whatever residual interest remained after those sports went into following rugby union's Wallabies. Soccer, and at this time it was known by no other name by the majority of Australians, was a sport for dilettantes—it wasn't fair dinkum. Channel Nine had given the sport a crack in 2002 and couldn't make it work. How could it when the local game's most marketable commodity, Harry Kewell, didn't even bother to come home and play for his country? The message from the naysayers was pretty clear: Fellas, have fun in Germany while it lasts but don't expect anything and don't get ahead of yourselves. Remember, we're Aussies—we're not like the rest of the world. Come June next year the only thing we'll be thinking about is Ricky Ponting getting back the Ashes. Once the World Cup's over, you won't have any pull. It'll be back to same old, same old.

Boy, did they get it wrong.

It's accepted by almost anyone who follows the game that football is an expression of national identity at its most stark; that the great teams and the way they play can be held up as a mirror of the societies they come from. It's a theory that holds with the Brazilians. They're flamboyant, athletic, always look like they're about to break out dancing. The same with the Italians. Touchy, self-absorbed, theatrical. The English are capable but dull, while the Croatians are hot-headed and brutal. The stereotypes—and they *are* stereotypes—are easy to identify and, though generalisations, have some basis in truth. So what, then, can be inferred about Australia from the Socceroos?

Prior to Christmas 2005, I thought I had it figured out: we unapologetically dish out the hard stuff, want to keep our structure at all times, can hold up the ball but fail up front when it matters most. In summary: we're battlers, capable of the big upset, can take direction, but often wilt under pressure or can't finish off an opponent. It's not gilding the lily to say Australia itself can be like that. We could be the greatest country in the world—many think we already are—but there's always something holding us back from taking *the next step.* Think of the Republic, reconciliation, signing the Kyoto Protocol, stem-cell research, federalism.

I'd also seen enough of rough-and-tumble Socceroos sides over two decades to accept that we weren't the most elegant of football nations. Graham Arnold's description of his own time playing for Australia under Frank Arok was of it being 'pretty much, "Let's get out there and scare the hell out of them"—our brand was to get by on the physical side of things'.

But that was precisely what I loved about the Australian team—they were always up against it. Football was one sport in which our supremacy wasn't a given. We frequently see athletes whose poor off-field behaviour is a symptom of a wider problem of excess and unaccountability in Australian sport. But the Socceroos, as far I was concerned, were a notable exception. They had carved out careers abroad in unfamiliar and sometimes hostile environments, proving they could thrive outside the bubble of Australian sporting celebrity with no special treatment, little media interest and, up until recent times, next to no support from administrators back home. They seemed genuinely touched when the mainstream media took the slightest bit of interest in what they were doing.

The prevailing attitude of the press even as recently as 2005 was that football was someone else's game. That attitude mystified me, and it certainly mystified people inside the sport. Among them was Socceroos captain Mark Viduka, who'd experienced the establishment's ingrained hostility not just as a kid in suburban Melbourne but as a world-class striker in the English Premier League. What did he have to do to make Australia sit up and take notice? He was exasperated by the indifference of his countrypeople.

'No other sport can generate this much interest and passion and patriotism,' he told me. 'This is the whole world. People who have loved soccer all their lives in Australia, we've all known that. Yet a lot of the time we've felt a little bit out of place because everybody around us was saying, "What's *this* game? It's a nil-all draw. What's the big deal?" What, people want a hundred goals a game or something to take it seriously?'

I particularly remember one day midway through 2005 when a new executive arrived at work, called me aside and asked me into his office. He closed the door. 'Things are going to be changing around here,' he said, putting his feet up on the table. He then proceeded to give me his prescription for the perfect sports magazine: milking every available drop out of our stable of 'local' sports stars, which meant a steady diet of rugby league, Aussie Rules and cricket, and no more Socceroos. His view was that a personality such as Adam Gilchrist, for instance, was worth at least three feature stories a year: one comparing him to the greats, one doing a 'dark side of' profile, and the other assessing his achievements over that calendar year. No room in the magazine, then, for Lucas Neill, Vince Grella, Viduka or anyone else in our national football team achieving such great things abroad. They were only to be written about if there was a match being played in Australia, or, when hell froze over, we made it to the World Cup.

Six months later, that prescription had been torn up. As the FFA liked to put it, 'old soccer' had become 'new football'. Middle Australia had embraced the Socceroos. John O'Neill counted the national team's securing of a sponsorship deal with cereal company Sanitarium as a big step towards mainstream acceptance. Such a statement might have irked the millions of parents who didn't need a blow-in from rugby to tell them the sport their kids played was now socially acceptable because Tim Cahill was on a Weet-Bix packet, but the message was not for them. It was for the ignorant pissants in the media, the TV programmers, the ad buyers, the corporate lunchers, the politicians who went where the wind blew. They were the ones who were out of step with the Australian public, not football.

Not everyone was a winner with Australian football kicking on, though. With the new guard being given the keys to the kingdom, many within the 'football family' now complained of being ignored; they railed privately that the FFA had been hijacked by greedy merchant bankers and tie-wearing lickspittles who had no respect for the history of the game and those who had built it. The house of football might have been a rundown old wreck before the FFA put it back on its foundations, but it was still *theirs.* Old Socceroos like the 1974 team's Ray Richards then went public, voicing their disdain for Frank Lowy's and O'Neill's cronies. Anything, so their sentiment ran, was better than what we had before Lowy and O'Neill hitched their wagons to the sport, but did the local game have to veer so far away from its traditional base just for the sake of fast dollars and AB demographic palatability?

Well, in short, yes. Thanks to a decisive kick in Sydney, Australia was now a player in the big bad world of international football. There was no looking back.

What convinced me the FIFA World Cup occupies another plane to all other sporting events was a report that came out of Thailand a few weeks before the tournament's opening match. The director-general of the country's Livestock Development Department, Yukol Limlaemthong, proudly announced that Germany 2006 had delivered a major fillip for Thai chicken exports. A World Cup, he said, was worth 20 per cent more sales to Japan and Europe. Impressive. If Thai chicken farmers could benefit that much from a four-week football tournament played far away in Germany, one in which Thailand wasn't even competing, what did the rest of the business world stand to gain?

Quite a bit. Ticket sales for Germany 2006 were over three million, and oversubscribed almost 30 times. The same number of foreign visitors turned up without a ticket. World Cup TV rights for the 2002 and 2006 tournaments sold for $3 billion, making the AFL's much ballyhooed $780 million TV rights deal for five years look like small change. Thirty billion people watched it on TV. Fifteen sponsors paid $50 million each to be an 'official partner'. The numbers go on and on and on.

Money, however, can only explain so much. You know a tournament is really something unique when it enters the sociological realm. Branko Milanovic, an economist at the Washington DC-based Carnegie Endowment for International Peace, argued in his essay 'Globalisation and Goals: Does $occer $how the Way?' in the *Review of International Political Economy* that football was responsible for the world's sole true 'globalised profession'—the transnational movement of football players from Africa, Asia and the Americas to Europe. With a global workforce at their disposal, the rich club sides of Europe—Barcelona, Bayern Munich, Manchester United, et al—were becoming superior and so success was shared by a privileged few. At the same time, national teams, especially those from Africa and South America, could now compete on a more level playing field at the World Cup because their players were being honed in better competitions. So while capitalism was making the gulf between champions and also-rans wider at club level, the World Cup itself was becoming more evenly balanced. The socialist ideal wasn't dead after all. It had found an unlikely home in the most capitalist sporting event on earth.

Time will tell if Milanovic is right, because in Germany the results wouldn't quite support his hypothesis. But his theory was basically sound. The World Cup, much more than the Olympics, has the power to touch almost every conceivable sector of humanity. In Europe, Russia, South America, Central America, West and East Asia, Africa and the Middle East, the *only* game is football, and the only competition that matters is the World Cup. Nothing else comes close. Even in cricket-besotted India, a country that has never been to a World Cup and probably never will, more than 50,000 people regularly turn out for games by East Bengal, one of the oldest and proudest football teams on the planet. In neighbouring Bangladesh, a cricketing country that can hardly play cricket, each World Cup divides the nation between Brazilian and Argentinean supporters' groups. Within 20 years, football will surely be as dominant in South Asia, North America and the Caribbean as it is everywhere else.

What about Australia? Why, when we've got Punter and Jodie and Lleyton all flying the flag and doing damn well, should we give ourselves over to another sport? Why should we sacrifice our precious time and our more precious nerves to a team of exiles we know will likely never be world champion?

A distinctive feature of Australian sport is its provincialism—we love sports where we can say, without hesitation, that we are the 'best in the world'. Hence our matchless passion for 10,000-metre swimming, rugby league, Aussie Rules—sports no one else really gives two hoots about. These sports provide a pedestal for national chest-beating, and serve to cement an illusion that we're more important on the global stage than we really are. USA coach Bruce Arena's comment before the World Cup that he thought Trinidad & Tobago and Australia were the two weakest teams in the tournament was offensive to a lot of Australian football supporters, but it was a view that was not uncommon overseas. After all, what had Australia done to deserve Arena's benefit of the doubt? Had we a record to match USA's World Cup appearances (eight), best ever result (semi-finalist in 1930), or goals scored (27)? There are a lot of historical reasons why American football had a better chance of proving itself on the world stage than our own, but the bald fact remained: We'd been to one World Cup and hadn't won a game. We were nobodies.

Of course, local football fans knew better than Arena and the large segment of the Australian population that still sneered at 'soccer'. They were used to getting bashed. Unlike their rugby league and Aussie Rules counterparts, they followed their sport not being able to see the 'best in the world' down at their local oval every weekend. Until recently, they'd had little choice but to support the football team of an ethnic social club or survive on whatever meagre rations of English or European league football were transmitted on SBS. Most, sensibly, opted for the latter. Late at night on those television sets in suburban lounge rooms, Australia's expatriate footballers were making quiet but significant steps for our country.

As globalisation became the new buzzword of the 1990s, it was no coincidence that rugby league and Aussie Rules began getting serious about national expansion and redefining their 'brands'.

Not because football was about to breach the ramparts, but because their very provincialism, what had formerly been the source of their strength, had suddenly become a liability. In the global marketplace, they would find themselves isolated. But where the indigenous sports of the United States were sustainable because of the country's vast economy of scale, Australia's indigenous sports were sitting ducks. League and Aussie Rules, through natural selection, were doomed. So today we see plans well advanced for the inaugural 20-team Australian Football World Cup in 2008, a tournament blessed with the AFL's imprimatur but without Australia competing, and the belated return from the wilderness of the longstanding but farcical Rugby League World Cup in the same year.

We are living in an age of unprecedented privilege but also uncertainty. We crave security—low interest rates, job protection, affordable petrol—yet, stripped of industry protection while our government champions free trade, all these things have become less guaranteed. This feeling of insecurity, of being unsure of what's going to happen next, runs counter to

Australia's embedded culture of surety, of being a winner in everything we do—especially in sport. So, in effect, the Socceroos are the team for this time in our nationhood. They might not be 'sure things', but they're the only team we can say are truly competing against the rest of the world. For this reason they represent for many people what has been an uncomfortable period of readjustment for Australia, a period in which we are being judged against global standards, not our own.

A year before he died, I had the privilege of interviewing Johnny Warren on the phone from his house in Jamberoo, south of Sydney. It was late 2003, and Warren wasn't well. He'd just returned from a cancer clinic in the United States, where he'd been trying to stave off another bout of the lung cancer that would eventually kill him.

Sometimes hectoring and overly emotional, Warren wasn't to everyone's taste, but I'd always been impressed with his outlook on life, enumerated in his appearances on the program *On the Ball,* an hour-long Sunday panel show that ran for a few years on SBS. Warren was a regular guest and liked to be upfront with his views, which didn't often accord with the game's administrators. This, of course, made it compulsive viewing. What I liked most about Warren, though, apart from his often unruly hair, was that he loved to bang on about South America, especially Brazil, a place he'd visited dozens of times and said he'd happily retire to, save for the family he had in Australia. It was obvious he wished he'd been born in Rio or Sáo Paulo. If for some reason viewers failed to pick up on his wanderlust, they couldn't miss the red and white Flamengo tracksuit he'd sometimes wear. (He would be cremated in it.)

Warren was an ordinary kid from the southern suburbs of Sydney who took a broad view of life: the world was bigger than Australia, England and America. Going on what we copped each day in newspapers or on the telly—saturation coverage of the AFL or NRL—most of the Australian sports media believed that nothing much existed beyond Sydney or Melbourne. It frustrated him that the world was out there waiting for Australia to join it, but that continually failing to qualify for the World Cup always scuppered his dream of making it happen. He was first diagnosed with cancer during Korea-Japan 2002, the last World Cup he would see. Back then, against all good sense, Australia was in the grip of a kind of World Cup fever.

'For the first time we were a real football country. That was such a buzz for us—for people like me—to see the whole of Australia football mad,' he said. 'I was a bit on about that [with God]. I just thought, well, "Why do you put me in that position then take it away from me?"'

Not everyone was caught up in the occasion. Like many in the football community, Warren kept tabs on what was being said about the sport in the mainstream press because it was the mainstream press that had to be won over if the game were ever to gain 'acceptance'. One commentator he particularly despised was the *Sydney Morning Herald* personality Peter FitzSimons, a former Wallabies forward who liked to make cracks at football's expense in 'The Fitz Files', his regular weekend sports column.

'Peter FitzSimons epitomises it. He epitomises the whole lot, the boofhead mentality that has a go at soccer,' Warren said. 'His commentary on soccer is a joke. Highlight the shit, but never mention it, you know. The media doesn't want to admit what our game is. I can't forget FitzSimons's comment before the World Cup: "What World Cup?" or something, he said ...'

Over a couple of hours, Warren riffed on all sorts of subjects, occasionally going off to answer a call from a friend or another journalist, and wasn't afraid to give an opinion when I asked for one. Because he was a man facing death, he was perhaps even more candid than usual, admitting to having contemplated suicide. But it was when I asked him what he thought was his greatest achievement that I was the most taken aback. It wasn't representing Australia at the 1974 World Cup in West Germany, or captaining the Socceroos, but 'travelling the world. Being part of a family, a global family, where if you're involved with the game you're welcomed, embraced as being part of it.' He pointed out that a club like Brazil's Flamengo, *his* team, a name largely unknown to Australian sports fans, had 30 million supporters.

'*Manyana* people' was how he described Australians. Brazilians, he said, lived for the day, the moment. Australians were too often thinking about tomorrow. If it doesn't happen now, there's always next time. *Manyana.* It was a philosophy that seemed to underpin generations of Socceroos teams, bar the trailblazing journey of Rale Rasic and his 1974 part-timers and a short burst of impressive results under Frank Arok in the 1980s. A draw was usually good enough. Failure was too often tolerated. Coaches and backroom staff who were well past their use-by dates were retained. If only Australia could get to the World Cup, all the problems would go away and soccer—football—would take its rightful place in Australia's sporting firmament. This was Warren's dream, but he knew he'd never see it in the short time he had left.

'Why are Australians so ignorant of South America?' he asked, not waiting for an answer. 'They would love it; they would *love* it. Whether you're Pelé or whether you play for the over-60 Jamberoo pub team, you're part of a family, a group, you have something in common. You sit down with a Pelé, who treats you with respect as a fellow player. I'm proud to be a part of that massive club worldwide. Our game is the world. Australia has to tap into what's happening in the world. That's our problem.'

Come June 2006, however, it would be our problem no more. Australia was about to hitch a ride with the Socceroos through a fortnight of football that would make us confront who we were and determine where we stood. Warren might have been long dead, but his wishes were finally being fulfilled.

CHAPTER TWO · THE HIDDINK SUPREMACY

'When I first started my coaching career ... I was like a nutcase ... I have to try to be cool. I'm rather passionate. I follow it ... I have to control myself to think that one or two steps ahead.'

GUUS HIDDINK,
IN AN INTERVIEW WITH DEREK RAE FOR ESPN'S
HEADLINERS: GUUS HIDDINK AND THE SOCCEROOS

Frank Lowy, fortunately, did not grow up with a *MANYANA* mentality. Spending his formative years fleeing Nazis and fighting a war in Palestine probably accounted for that. If he had grown up in the Australia of Ben Chifley or Robert Menzies, his life might have taken a very different turn. The Socceroos might not have made it to Germany 2006.

After all, what sort of man spikes the national coach three months out from a World Cup qualifying two-leg playoff, with no one to step into the breach? Someone, obviously, who wants to get things done and isn't about to wait around for someone else to do it. Perhaps, too, like Johnny Warren, Lowy was keenly aware of his own mortality. For a man nearing 80, a workaholic who slept just a few hours a night, he wasn't known for his patience.

I'd crossed paths with Lowy on a number of occasions, the last time at the Confederations Cup in Frankfurt in mid-2005. By pure coincidence he was staying at the same hotel as me, the grand Steigenberger Frankfurter Hof (I could afford to because

Gerhard Schröder was picking up the tab).

Lowy had been FFA chairman for some time, but here in Frankfurt was the first occasion he'd been in the company of FIFA's leaders and illuminati. The first time I'd met the Westfield titan, in 2001, we'd chatted briefly about football. He told me he liked going to English Premier League matches when in London.

'So any plans to return to Australian football, Frank?' I'd ventured, half-jokingly. He'd pulled his own club, Sydney City, out of the National Soccer League (NSL) in 1987 and abandoned the game altogether to concentrate on his shopping-centre interests.

'No,' he said, smiling. 'I don't have the time. I am too busy. I love the game but there are too many problems. There is too much politics. I have no reason to go back. You never say never, but I don't want to get involved again.'

In Frankfurt, I didn't remind him of that conversation. It felt like a million years had elapsed. Lowy had indeed come back—in a spectacular way. After concerted pushing and prodding from various factions, he'd had a change of heart and was here in this chintzy hotel in southern Germany, with the FFA's John O'Neill, John Boultbee and Matt Carroll and half a dozen Fijians I'd never seen before in my life, to try to get Australia's campaign for the World Cup back on track and his federation into Asia.

The reasons for his backflip were complex but also remarkably prosaic. Lowy had spent his life reading from the same script as Warren: Tap into what's happening in the world. Embrace it. Don't shun it. Australia's wealthiest self-made man was international to the core, a melange of European, Israeli, Australian and American life experience. His own story had been full of twists and diversions, adventures and follies, but no matter how rich and powerful he became, no matter where he was in the world, he was always grounded by football, the sport he'd begun following as a small boy under the influence of his father, Hugo, in the Slovakian-Hungarian border town of Filakovo. Then, he'd been penniless. Now he was one of the 200 richest men in the world, but he retained the same boyish enthusiasm for the minutiae of the game.

We talked about why Tim Cahill had been taken off by Frank Farina in the match against Germany, when it was clear he'd been one of the few players who looked capable of scoring an equaliser. The others in his group seemed to think Farina had made the right call. Lowy just shook his head. He'd long ago made up his mind about the national coach—having met 'many coaches, probably about ten' before Hiddink was chosen. However the performance in Frankfurt suddenly became a convenient rationale for the decision that would come at the end of the tournament. Farina was purged.

'I wanted to do it beforehand, but [the performance at the Confederations Cup] doubled the effort to find somebody else,' he said.

Three losses in three games was an embarrassing return for the FFA, especially when Lowy had been in Germany talking up the benefits Australia would bring to Asia. Unlike his predecessors as chairman, Lowy didn't see why it was necessary to put up with an Aussie coach who failed when there were better candidates out there who could do the job the first time. Nor did it deter him that there were only a few months before the all-important playoffs between Australia and the fifth-placed South American team.

Lowy could be that confident because he had a very special person in mind for the task—PSV Eindhoven's Guus Hiddink, the only man to lead two separate nations to the semi-final stage of the World Cup. His name had been mentioned in passing years before by family friend and FFA board director Phillip Wolanski. Lowy had paid careful attention.

'When I [became chairman] I made enquiries around the world. I have some contacts in Holland and they found his agent [Cees van Nieuwenhuizen] and he introduced me to Hiddink,' said Lowy. 'I had a dinner with him in Amsterdam about a month after I had taken the job. I looked around where I could find a coach, because I felt it was essential for us to succeed. It took about a year or two to negotiate with him to join us.'

Hiddink's recruitment, however, was never a *fait accompli*. Other candidates were still in the mix right up until the moment pen signed paper. Graham Arnold, who Farina begged to stay on as assistant coach for the sake of the country's World Cup mission, met ex-Dutch national coach Dick Advocaat for an hour in London and was then flown to Holland, where he was kept in the dark about who he was about to meet until Van Nieuwenhuizen picked him up at Eindhoven airport. Van Nieuwenhuizen turned to Arnold and cut straight to the chase: 'There's only one person who can stuff this deal up and it's you. If you don't sell it to him he'll walk away.'

'Hiddink had in his contract that he wouldn't sign anything until he had spoken to me about the football side of things—players, programs and going forward—so I basically had to sell him the job,' said Arnold. 'I sat with him alone for a half hour in a side room at the airport Novotel, just me and him, and he said, "Tell me why I should take this." I convinced him we had the players with the desire and showed him the program we had ahead. He'd seen the Confederations Cup, and he saw what he believed were our problems. Guus asked me what I thought our problems were and I told him and we agreed. He said, "Right, I've heard enough."'

Arnold signed and witnessed the contract and the two men toasted the deal over champagne.

When Hiddink's appointment was made official that July, it was a clear sign, if any were needed, that the old rules of engagement and small-minded provincialism in Australian football no longer applied. Lowy's net had been cast wide. Here was one of the world's best coaches, a man adaptable to any culture, east or west, standing outside the Sydney Opera House to pose for pictures that would be seen within seconds on the other side of the world. It was a serious statement of intent. It also demonstrated the significance of the adventure on which Australia was about to embark. A World Cup, even a World Cup qualifying campaign, is no place for chumps. If we were going to get to Germany, we were going to do it not by half measures but by embracing the best the world had to offer—even if we could only get Hiddink on a part-time basis. He had agreed to the terms only on the condition he retained his club contract and led Australia to the World Cup when his schedule allowed.

The importance Hiddink placed on managing his time was immediately apparent to Arnold. For three days after the contract signing, he was forced to hang around PSV's training ground, taking walks with Australia's new coach during breaks. Though impressed by Hiddink's breadth of knowledge about Australia's players and their respective strengths, he wasn't kidding himself that his new boss was about to reinvent the wheel for Australian football.

'Guus was very fortunate that he was able to take over a stable team,' he told me. 'Frank Farina had been in charge, with myself, for five years, and the core of the team was the same for that time, so the group was very stable, focused and hungry. Hiddink only worked 24 days for us [between signing his contract and the Uruguay game], so a lot of the groundwork had already been done by Farina. The difference was Hiddink had a lot of experience. He came in with no baggage. He could probably make decisions blindly that other people wouldn't have made. Like leaving Harry Kewell on the bench against Uruguay. If Frank had done that, and it didn't work, he would have got killed.'

The rationale behind that decision, Arnold explained, was not to unleash Kewell on an unsuspecting Uruguay or piss off Australia's greatest football talent, but to protect the team's most valuable asset from being physically assaulted and put out of the game by the hard-playing South Americans. Hiddink's thinking was that once the Uruguayans had fatigued from the usual helter-skelter opening stoushes of a sudden-death World Cup qualifier, Kewell would be given the freedom he needed to perform.

'I'll never forget what Hiddink said: "With my experience, you never win these games in the first 20 minutes, half hour. You only lose them." So we started with an extra defender, Tony Popovic. Everything that you saw was pre-planned, that Harry was on the bench, he was going to come on after 35, 40 minutes ... it got sped up a little bit by Popovic throwing the elbow. Straight away, Hiddink said, "Just get him off. Don't even worry about Harry not being warm, just get him off. Because they'll search [Popovic], look for another yellow, and he's gone." So we just dragged Tony off before Harry was ready.'

Minutes later, Kewell had set up the goal that would tie the two-leg playoff series and send the match into extra-time and penalties. And so history was made.

The real test of the Dutchman's necromantic powers, however, would come *after* Uruguay were beaten. What kind of team would Australia take to the park against Zico's Japan on 12 June in Kaiserslautern and what sort of football would they be playing?

After the Sydney game, Hiddink flew back to Europe and returned to his day job, taking Socceroos Jason Culina and Archie Thompson with him, the latter's signing causing a mini-crisis for the fledgling domestic competition, the A-League. Not much would happen in the national coaching position for a few months.

But by late February 2006, it was time for the nucleus of his squad to come together again. Hiddink audaciously scrapped a planned friendly against Colombia in England and arranged for 14 players to convene in Mierlo, outside Eindhoven, for a three-day camp. For many in the squad, it was the first real opportunity they'd had to savour the team's qualification in the cold light of day—as well as bond over a game or two of tennis.

'Everyone was looking forward to going into camp to catch up,' said Mark Bresciano. 'They're a good bunch of boys and we're all good friends. Other than training we just hung around, having coffee, drinking. We were very close before but obviously our achievements brought the group closer.'

The only other World Cup country not to play a friendly that week was Togo. Australians wouldn't see their national football team on home soil until the Greece game in Melbourne on 25 May. They were lucky to get that.

Hiddink had his work cut out. Not just in the formidable challenge that lay ahead in Germany but in getting his players to comprehend what he had in store for them. Unlike many of our celebrated national teams—the Australian cricketers and the Wallabies are two examples—the Socceroos had for decades existed in a state of flux. There was minimal continuity in personnel, strategy, training programs or, at the most basic level, in time spent together. A Ricky Stuart in league or a John Connolly in rugby inherits a group of players who know one another's playing styles intimately, who socialise together and live in one or two cities on the eastern seaboard of Australia. Pecking orders are established and implicitly understood. The Socceroos were different. Their team culture had always depended on who was in charge or what players were available that week. Hiddink, though, as he had done while coach of Holland and Korea, made it clear that reputations counted for nothing. What he saw with his own eyes was the only thing that mattered. The side would be picked according to what happened on the training ground. His man-management would be crucial. Players would have to accept they might be yanked from the park at any minute or not used at all, a strategy that would alienate some members of the team. Above all, his most important requirement was solidarity. Hiddink's squad would go to Germany united and committed, representing not only the best players he could assemble, but also, if we were to swallow the hype, the idea of Australia itself.

'Guus is a great guy,' Lucas Neill told me just prior to the World Cup. Australia's central defender was on a beach in Dubai, catching some sun before going into camp again in Holland. 'He came in and obviously was trying to feel out the personalities of each and every one of us. He's a good judge of character, so he was quick to learn about certain people, and just from his resume in the world of football he commanded respect. Guus has a charisma about him. Immediately he opens his mouth and it makes sense, and as a result everybody listens. You listen because you know he's going to give you something you've never heard before. He's got that World Cup kind of magic about him.

'When we get into the [team camp] dining room we're all leaders. There's no captain, no one's funnier than anyone else, no one thinks they're better than anyone else. There are no stars, even though we've got Harry, Dukes and Bresh, Schwarzer and Cahill. Everybody's on the same level. Everybody gets the piss taken out of them, everybody laughs at jokes and everybody has jokes made about them. The most important thing is Guus won't take sides and he won't treat anyone differently. Look at Harry [in the Sydney World Cup qualifier]. He just dropped him, because the team was more important than Harry. That pissed Harry off—I know because we roomed together—and it got exactly what we needed out of him. That's why Guus is what he is.'

Not everybody was in thrall of the self-described 'Dutch farmer boy'. That much became apparent in the only player diary that appeared following the World Cup. In *Mark Schwarzer's World Cup Destiny: From Sydney to Stuttgart*, Australia's number one carefully couched his language but painted a picture of a head coach who played cruel 'psychological games' with his players. Schwarzer, especially, was left feeling tormented on the eve of important games, not knowing if he would play even when he felt he had done everything on the training pitch he needed to do and had the match fitness to get the edge on his rival, Zeljko Kalac. Indeed, the fact that the Socceroos' goalkeeping position was kept open before and during the World Cup marked Hiddink as a very different beast to his contemporaries. In the German team, for instance, Jürgen Klinsmann named Jens Lehmann as his number one well before the tournament, leaving veteran custodian Oliver Kahn enough time to deal with his disappointment and cool down. France coach Raymond Domenech had done the same when he named Fabien Barthez over Gregory Coupet. But not Hiddink.

I tried to contact Hiddink after the World Cup to ask him about the rationale behind his goalkeeper selection, but his Dutch representatives refused an interview: 'Guus Hiddink is going to publish his own book. In this book there will be several chapters about Australia and the World Cup and I am sorry to inform you that Guus Hiddink will not be able to talk to you.' When the ghostwritten tome, *Dit Is Mijn Wereld* (*This Is My World*) was released in Europe in November 2006, Hiddink played it characteristically straight: 'I really wasn't convinced that either of them could do a great job.'

Arnold, who saw the saga unfold up close, felt the matter was poorly handled by Schwarzer.

'By the time we got to the World Cup, Guus wanted to get extra out of everyone,' he said. 'He was very hard on people and players. Whether I could have done that, I don't know. I don't think so. But he wanted to challenge them all. I know what Mark has said, but that's maybe because Mark comes from a different environment where everything is explained to him. But Guus was like, "We're at the *World Cup*. Jesus Christ, we're playing for our country. There's 23 of us, it's not about 11. It's about 23 plus the staff. We have to make decisions and [you players] are playing for your country at the World Cup."'

South Korea's assistant coach Afshin Ghotbi, who worked as a technical analyst for Hiddink at Korea-Japan 2002, assured me Hiddink's handling of the goalkeeping issue was no accident.

The same thing had happened in Seoul four years before.

'In all the friendlies we had before the 2002 World Cup what Guus would do was alternate the two 'keepers—the younger one who wasn't a star versus the one that was,' he said. 'He literally waited until the last few days before the tournament to decide what 'keeper he was going with. I think he made the right choice. The goalkeeper turned out to be Lee Woon-jae, now over 100 caps, probably the best 'keeper in Asia. He put in a great performance in 2002. I think if he had gone with just the one 'keeper, and let everyone know in advance which one it was, he wouldn't have got the same performance out of Woon-jae. Guus did what he thought he had to do to get that out of him.'

Craig Foster is an astute football analyst. Get him talking about the game on a slow news day and it's like trying to stop a burst water main with a tampon. When we caught up after Germany 2006, I asked for his view of how the goalkeeper situation had played out and what challenges beyond man-management Hiddink had faced in fashioning a competitive team.

'Hiddink wasn't convinced about Schwarzer and neither was I. Schwarzer's always got the ability to make a stupid mistake, he's made them on a number of occasions for Australia,' he told me. 'I don't put him in world-class category at all. The reason Hiddink didn't back him as number one was because he *wasn't* his number one. He was never sure about him.

'In the past, we've just been a team who had to get it forward as early as possible. Highly predictable stuff. It was no good Hiddink trying to keep Australia as a counter-attacking nation, because we're not. We're—as [Fédération Française de Football technical director] Aimé Jacquet said—dynamic athletes. We've got good mental competitive characteristics, which means we want to take the game to people; that's why the team resonated so much under Terry Venables and now under Hiddink. They're the two managers that came in and said: "We're going to attack teams."

'One of the first things Hiddink said to the boys was: "We're gonna defend from the front, get away from our goal." The Dutch are the absolute antithesis of the way we played [under Farina]. They value possession, which we could never achieve. They play high up the park when we would play defensively—we'd sit on our box. They'd use fast ball circulation and passing to move defences around. We'd just get it forward. Everything we weren't under Farina, basically.'

With almost every team in Germany able to play technically proficient football, what advantage had Australia taken into the tournament, if any? Had being Australian itself factored in our chances?

'Hiddink identified our national character better than Eddie Thomson ever did,' Foster said. 'Thomson's character was the Scottish national character. Hiddink's character from a football sense is a lot closer to where Australia *wants* to be. We recognise what quality football is. There's many nations in the world who just want to win and they don't care how they do it. Australians aren't like that.'

Could we really differentiate ourselves when it came to kicking a ball around a park?

Hiddink thought we could. He spoke of Australia's 'huge mental force' but qualified that praise by saying there was 'no balance between the effort and the cleverness of play'. The key to getting the best out of the Aussies was to strike a balance between their natural instincts—to fight, to scrap, to never give up—with a bit of Dutch intelligence. In Mierlo in March, in among the ribaldry and team-bonding, some serious work was being done: two two-hour structural sessions a day for ten days straight, many of those without a ball.

The Socceroos would have to learn quickly. This pre-World Cup window would be the players' only chance to learn from the master, because by mid-April Hiddink's wily agent Van Nieuwenhuizen had confirmed what the FFA had feared: that the Football Union of Russia had come in with a massive salary and bonuses package, bankrolled by Chelsea's billionaire owner Roman Abramovich, to lure Australia's new coach to Moscow once the World Cup was over. His last day in the job would be whenever Australia was knocked out.

It was a soft blow, as it hadn't been unexpected, but it did create an awkward vacuum within the national team before they arrived in Germany. Arnold and fellow assistant Johan Neeskens, both former internationals with limited club coaching experience, began lobbying for the top job as a duo even before a ball had been kicked. This sideshow became more disruptive when Hiddink intervened to lend them his support, telling reporters when the squad flew back to Mierlo in late May that the FFA was stupid to 'waste money' on snaring another first-tier coaching appointment, such as Lowy's favoured candidate, Olympique Lyonnais's Gérard Houllier. The FFA chairman didn't bite. It was left to Van Nieuwenhuizen to announce publicly that Lowy's flat rejection of the Neeskens-Arnold pairing had compelled his client to rule out a return to Australian football after his Russia contract expired in 2008, a threat since relaxed. Australia's second-richest man was probably not used to having his hand bitten by someone he was feeding with hundred-dollar bills, but until Australia went out of the World Cup, only one man was calling the shots and that was Hiddink.

The media pack following the Socceroos had had that spelled out loud and clear. If they'd thought they'd get to share a few steins with Harry Kewell and Tim Cahill at the bar of the ritzy Wald und Schlosshotel in the woods of Friedrichsruhe, they were sadly deluded. Fraternising with players or team staff was forbidden. Following the Socceroos would not be like a Kangaroos tour of Great Britain. Anything but.

Hiddink had learned some valuable lessons from his mentor, Rinus Michels, FIFA's 'Coach of the Century', whose 1974 *Oranje* had been expected to blitz the tournament—and did—but self-destructed in the final. Their uncharacteristically insipid performance that day was blamed on German magazine *Bild Zeitung* publishing a story about an alleged sex romp at the team hotel pool on the eve of the match. The Dutch had never quite got over their failure and Hiddink would not repeat the mistake. He'd clamped down hard on out-of-control egos coaching Holland at France '98 and never let his South Korean team in 2002 feel totally settled.

'Hiddink's objective was always to win,' explained Ghotbi. 'Psychology is one of the most important things in football—how you deal with players, the atmosphere in the locker-room, the atmosphere in training, the atmosphere prior to matches. That is the key to success. Guus really understood that. There were times he shared information, times when he didn't. Sometimes he was confrontational, others he was very passive in his approach. He used whatever methods he needed to get results for the team.'

Those methods had some sort of payoff—both sides had reached the penultimate stage of the tournament. So for the Socceroos in Germany, aiming to make it three in a row for their new gaffer, their time under the 'old-fashioned' Hiddink would require total discipline. No sex. No drugs. No parties. No yacking on mobile phones. And certainly no media distractions. Whether the Aussies could hack it was another matter entirely.

'Korean players are very different to Australian or European players,' said Ghotbi. 'You can have them train three or four times a day, you can take them to the top of the mountain and have them run forever and they don't really complain. They just do what they're asked to do. With Korea, Guus rarely was confrontational with the big-name players. Very clever. Almost like a poker player in that he never showed his hand. No decisions were made. He'd wait till the last moment to select players. He would literally sit at meals and look at players' body language, their physical demeanour, which of them had the positive mental energy, who was sharp on that particular day. Ask anyone who's been in football long enough: the players that play rarely complain about the manager. The players who don't play or who aren't selected complain. Players have to adapt to Guus's management style because at the end of the day he's the boss.'

So without scoops on who might be in the team or what tactics were on the whiteboard, the media pack was reduced to simple observation for gathering intelligence. But divining any secrets from the Greece friendly at home or the Socceroos' warm-up games against Holland and Liechtenstein would prove a quixotic assignment. What sort of team Hiddink was preparing to unveil in Kaiserslautern was anyone's guess.

The Greece match was more a valedictory celebration than a rigorous contest, the European champions a far cry from the squad that had crushed Portugal in their own backyard, but the Australians, directed expertly by Jason Culina, Vince Grella and Mark Bresciano, played to a plan and stuck to it all game. Their dominance never looked like being challenged, but worryingly the only score came through a moment of opportunism from Josip Skoko.

On 4 June, under blue skies in the port city of Rotterdam, Marco van Basten's *Oranje* provided a more telling gauge of Hiddink's progress with his new team. Holland was in the middle of a golden period, Van Basten having taken them through qualifying unbeaten. There was talk this *Oranje* could go one further than Hiddink's in '98, but the Dutch, the World Cup's most resigned bridesmaids, had learned not to tempt fate. Cruel endings were an accepted part of the country's football narrative, as David Winner wrote in *Brilliant Orange: The Neurotic Genius of Dutch Football,* a state of affairs brought about by 'a quintessentially Dutch combination of ill-discipline, complacency, and lack of will or nerve. The Dutch seem to have an allergy to authority, leadership and collective discipline.'

Against the Socceroos, though, they were raging favourites and they knew it. Holland took to the field looking like clones of Robert Patrick's T-1000 robot in *Terminator II: Judgment*

Day—all height, jaw and sinew—and pulverised the Socceroos, controlling possession, dictating the tempo and defending in packs. They gave the hapless Aussies no time to find their bearings, no time to look up from their feet. Australian passes were being sprayed everywhere. First touches were abysmal, especially from Grella and bench player Luke Wilkshire, a bolter in the squad who'd been granted a rare start. The team's lack of pace was also exposed, Brett Emerton, the Socceroos' most agile player, being run ragged down the flanks by Chelsea's Arjen Robben. If a wakeup call were needed, this first 45 minutes at De Kuip, 'The Tub', had provided it.

When the Socceroos came out after the break they were a different team, unafraid to play to their strengths but maintaining their concentration and skill level. Even after the nervous Wilkshire got sent off and the Aussies went down to ten men, they kept a throathold-like grip on the Dutch from which the home team never recovered. The end result, a 1-1 draw, was ultimately flattering, but it was also a declaration to the world that Australia wasn't going to Germany to pussyfoot around. Van Basten described the carnage in his dressing-room as 'like an episode of *M*A*S*H*'. The match reports didn't pull punches, either. The Aussies were physical brutes playing a style of football that would win them no friends. This, however, was progress. Whatever the Germans would have us believe, World Cups aren't the time to make friends.

Yet just three days later against Liechtenstein, a team ranked 123 in the world and Europe's equivalent of Hutt River Province, the Socceroos tanked. The only real positive to emerge in an unconvincing 3-1 win was Harry Kewell, crocked since his FA Cup cameo, returning to the field with a new hairdo and lasting an hour. The hordes of Aussie fans following the team, camped in their motorhomes or taking in the sights before the serious business of Japan got underway, could have been forgiven for feeling some trepidation.

Lucas Neill, Australia's rock at the back who'd let in an uncharacteristic own goal in Ulm, understood better than most what confronted his team in a few days' time in Kaiserslautern. Some members of the Australia squad were calling the game their 'World Cup final'. With Craig Moore, Neill was the player whose split-second decisions against Hidetoshi Nakata and Shunsuke Nakamura would mean the difference between tournament survival and extinction. Yet he wasn't shirking from the challenge. If anything, he couldn't wait.

'If we win, it opens up so many options for us,' he told me. 'But if we draw it makes it tough, and if we lose then we're really, really fighting against it. We need to hit the ground running. Every game is going to be an upset if we win, as far as the football world is concerned. If we get four or five upsets, we'll find ourselves well and truly up there. We're confident we're going to have a fantastic three weeks, not just two.'

No one, however, was rebooking their flights just yet.

CHAPTER THREE · KOKODA

'We are in a very tough group. Croatia and Brazil are very good.'

JAPAN COACH ZICO, 2006

Everywhere I looked, there were girls on bicycles. Beautiful girls in the full bloom of youth, hair trailing in the wind, carefree, whistling Edith Piaf songs en route to romantic assignations with fine-boned poets with immaculate hair and unblemished skin. That's at least how I saw it. It was hard not to get swept up in the romance of Strasbourg, France's most eastern city and capital of the new, freewheeling Europe.

I had an excellent view of the action: a fourth-floor apartment in the centre of town overlooking the main square, Place Kléber. I had chosen to come here with my family and a few close friends because it seemed the best place to spend our time during the World Cup—close enough to Germany to be able to commute to Australia's games, but far enough away to stand a fair chance of ingesting anything other than *currywurst mit pommes frites* for two weeks. Germany was just a five-minute drive from the city centre, yet once in Kehl, the industrial town on the other side of the turpid Rhine, there was no mistaking what you had left behind.

Being based on the border seemed the smart option, but when I first told colleagues back home where I was staying they were confused. Wasn't the World Cup in Germany? Yes, but Strasbourg was unique. Not only could you see the German influence in the half-timbered houses and the street signs in two languages, but unlike every other French city, where dog shit is considered a major social problem, Strasbourg's streets were so clean you could almost see your reflection in them. Being so close to Germany but not *in* Germany had its advantages.

It had plenty of disadvantages too, not least the fact that because of its geographical position in the armpit of France and Germany, Strasbourg had been a plaything for armies for centuries. In 1949, British foreign secretary Ernest Bevin had been moved to call it the city that 'more than any other, has been the victim of the stupidity of the nations of Europe which thought they could solve their problems by waging war'.

He'd spoken with some intimate knowledge of the subject. Just a few years before, the city and its surrounding areas had been overrun with Nazis. Strasbourg had been one of the first cities to fall to the Wehrmacht in the early days of the war and became an important symbol in Hitler's conquest of France. It was in Place Kléber, renamed Karl Roos Platz after a German-sympathising Alsatian who had been murdered by the French, that the Nazis staged mass rallies and tore down a statue of Napoleonic general Jean-Baptiste Kléber, the hero of Egypt. For good measure, they also disinterred his corpse. Today, over 60 years later, General Kléber was standing on his plinth again but trust between the two countries had been harder to restore. In Strasbourg, a glib slogan like 'A Time to Make Friends' had sinister connotations.

The tragic story of the city could be told through its football team. Racing Club de Strasbourg had originally started out as a German team, FC Neudorf, but took a French name after the Treaty of Versailles in 1919. When Hitler invaded France in 1940, the team became a crucible for the French resistance. The local league was disbanded and replaced with a new German competition. Forced to re-become German, Racing now called itself Rasensport Club Strasbourg (RCS) and its players were obliged to give the Hitler salute at matches. Racing's crosstown rival, Red Star Strasbourg, fared even worse. It was taken over by the German secret police and renamed Sportgeimeinschaft SS Strasbourg.

SS tried to blackmail RCS's best players with threats of imprisonment in a concentration camp, drafting into the Wehrmacht, or death. Some submitted; others, like Oskar Rohr, a German who had played with Bayern Munich and was Racing's top striker, refused. He fled to southwest France, joined the French Foreign Legion against the Nazis, was captured, and saw out the war in a concentration camp. Rohr's team-mates, though, were not about to surrender without a fight, contriving more subtle ways of bucking the Germans. They sang French songs in their locker-room and, during one game in 1942, defeated SS wearing a red, blue and white strip. Infuriated, the Nazis subsequently decreed only two colours could ever be worn.

SS did not survive the war, but Racing did, and today there was no mistaking its paternity. Its playing roster was as multicultural as France itself—Cameroonians, Moroccans, Ivorians, Egyptians, Tunisians, Senegalese. In the spirit of the *république*, France coach Raymond Domenech had picked 17 black or 'coloured' players in his squad of 23 for the World Cup. In contrast, Germany's Jürgen Klinsmann had picked two.

The map suggested it was pretty straightforward. Get on the A4 north of Strasbourg, cross the border at Wissembourg and take the back roads through the vineyards and the Pfälzerwald Naturpark to Kaiserslautern. The scenic route.

Two of the blokes sharing our flat, Neil 'Jamo' Jameson, a sportswriter and football nut, and his mate Keith 'Harro' Harris, a white-haired bear of a man who'd once laced up as a striker for Newcastle KB United in the old NSL, hadn't been convinced. This was their first World Cup, and they'd wanted to get to the Socceroos' opening match as quickly as possible, even if it meant missing out on the countryside.

Certainly sightseeing wasn't their top priority. They'd turned up in matching 'AUSTRALIA' shirts the previous morning after getting a train from Paris, made their introductions, then found a table at the local bar, ordered the first round of many beers, and didn't move away from the plasma TV until after the last game that day, Angola vs Portugal. They then came back to the apartment, somewhat pie-eyed, and watched the highlights before crashing at about 2 am. I'm not sure if they were still hungover, but the next morning they acceded to my plan without a word of dissent.

In the rearview mirror of our Renault, though, it was clear from Jamo's inflamed cheeks and Harro's stony stare that they'd wished they'd spoken up. Somehow we'd all left Strasbourg without first learning how to get the car in reverse and, one wrong turn later, were now stuck in a cul-de-sac in the French village of Hagenau, 30 kilometres north of the city and miles from any autobahn. Every time I moved the gearstick to where 'R' was, it inched forward instead. There were just two centimetres between the front number plate and a stone wall.

This was not how I'd planned our first trip to the World Cup. Worse, there didn't seem to be anyone around who could help. Where was everybody in Hagenau? Working in the fields? Crushing grapes? In the 20 minutes it took to figure out the problem (a small latch had to be raised under the head of the gearstick), the only local to come to our aid was a hunchbacked octogenarian peasant in a grey felt hat. After our sign-language French failed to elicit any sympathy, he just shrugged his shoulders and walked away.

Back on the road to the border, we'd lost valuable time. The silence in the back was excruciating. Perhaps music would help improve the mood? In preparation for the trip, I'd burned a mix CD featuring classic Australian songs such as Men at Work's 'Overkill' and the Sunnyboys' 'Alone With You', with selected highlights of Peter Wilkins's call of the playoffs in Montevideo and Sydney. ('He took a DIVE, appealed for the PENALTY. The referee stayed COOL. He said NO. Is that going to impact on the whole SCENARIO at the CENTENARIO?' Classic stuff from Wilko.)

I put it on and it had no effect; in fact, it seemed to aggravate Jamo and Harro. Even when we reached the vineyards of Wissembourg and I pointed out a sign for 'Winegut Cuntz', it barely raised a chuckle.

'Let's just get to Kaiserslautern,' growled Jamo.

I slammed my foot on the accelerator and prayed we'd make it before kickoff.

The 'Samurai Blue' hardly needed extra motivation to beat the Socceroos. Japan, after all, was taking on a team coached by Guus Hiddink. Four years before, the Japanese had been eclipsed by their neighbours and co-hosts across the strait. Japan had done all right, reaching the second round, but Korea had done better, reaching the last four—Asia's best ever result. It hurt Japan that the 2002 tournament would be remembered as Korea's, so this was a chance to get one back against Hiddink and restore face.

Japan certainly looked up to it by reputation. Their coach in 2002, eccentric Frenchman Philippe Troussier, who'd been described by one Japanese journalist as 'stable as uranium', had left his post and was now living as a Muslim under the *nom de guerre* of Omar in Morocco. His stabler replacement was Arthur Antunes Coimbra, better known to the world as Zico.

The grey but still handsome Brazilian—the great striker of the 1982 and 1986 World Cups—had inherited much more than a tight professional unit from Troussier. Football had gone on to become bigger than baseball and sumo in Japan and the national team had won the past two Asian Cups. The Japan Football Association (JFA) had successfully adopted a French-style youth development system, technical levels were advanced, and many top-shelf Brazilian players were earning big money in the domestic competition, the J. League. Zico himself had been one of the first former *Seleção*, 'Selection', to finish his playing career in the east. There he had been admired for his tireless work rate and passion for winning.

In *Japanese Rules*, his account of the creation of the J. League, Sebastian Moffett described how during the competition's inaugural season Zico's team Kashima Antlers met Kawasaki Verdy (later renamed Tokyo Verdy 1969) in a two-leg playoff. Verdy won the first game 2-0 and then in the final few minutes of the second, with Kashima ahead 1-0 and searching for an all-important extra, Verdy's Brazilian midfielder Paulo dived in the penalty area and was awarded a direct free kick.

'It was all too much for Zico,' wrote Moffett. 'He had come out of retirement, played in the second division of Japan's corporate amateur league, then built up the Antlers to be one of Japan's best teams ... but now, just before the moment that would justify all this effort, a referee was about to take it away. Zico walked up to the ball. He bent over it, as if to check it was properly on the spot—and spat.'

Referee Shizuo Takada, who had already handed out one yellow to the fiery Brazilian striker, had no choice but to show him a second and send him off. It was only the fifth time in a 25-year playing career that Zico had been given his marching orders.

J. League chairman Saburo Kawabuchi was aghast: 'It was as if he had spat at the J. League itself.' But Zico wasn't about to apologise: 'Since I came to Japan, I have always put my heart and soul into it. I didn't want to be another foreign player who didn't do enough, and I did not let up once.'

Yet for all their coach's inexhaustible reserves of grit, there was no escaping three incontrovertible facts for Japan's national football team: they were devoid of quality strikers; only six squad members were playing in Europe (and then only sparingly, being mostly used off the bench); and almost to a man they were a good head shorter than the Australians. All this, combined with fear of Australia's rough play—Kawabuchi, now JFA chief, had labelled the Australians a bunch of reprobates who committed a 'lot of dirty fouls' and liked to 'target ankles'—meant that despite outward signs of cockiness in the country's media, the Japanese were understandably apprehensive going into their opening game against the Socceroos.

More worryingly for Japan, their lead-up form had been poor. In qualifying, they'd hardly had to break a sweat in beating Oman, Singapore, India, North Korea, Iran and Bahrain, losing just once, in the unforgiving Azadi Stadium in Tehran. But when they played the vastly overrated USA in San Francisco, employing a 3-6-1 formation to make the most of their disproportionate talent in midfield—Shinji Ono, Hidetoshi Nakata and Shunsuke Nakamura were the team's undisputed star players—they lost easily. Yet rather than admit his team selection—and his tactics—were faulty, Zico blamed 'inappropriate shoes' (he is famously obsessive about footwear, having played in other people's boots when he was young and poor in Brazil). A 2-1 loss to Bulgaria at home followed, a game in which the Samurai Blue had 20 shots at goal, and a scoreless draw with an inept Scotland saw them surrender the three-team Kirin Cup.

The Japanese public's World Cup expectations and their team's World Cup prospects weren't on the same page. Hiddink, though, was not risking complacency, pointing out to Australian journalists in March that the Japanese weren't the only nation with a mortgage on fighting spirit, *yamato damashi.*

Not all the seats had been filled at kickoff, but the well-marshalled Japanese fans made the 46,000 capacity feel more like 96,000, booming the solitary word 'NI-PPON!' followed by three claps for most of the game. It was easy to admire the Zen perfunctoriness of it. These *oendan,* or support groups, are an ingrained part of Japanese culture, where for many students supporting a team is regarded as an honourable alternative to playing sport at high school and university. The motley Australian fans, perhaps stunned by the 38°C heat or the fog of BO (tournament volunteers had confiscated all deodorant at the gate), didn't seem to know how to respond to the wall of noise. 'Waltzing Matilda' didn't quite work as a gee-up, 'C'mon Aussie,

C'mon!' was inappropriate for a football match, and 'You Only Sing When You're Whaling' was funny but not exactly original: it had been pinched from the Scots, who had taunted Norway fans with it at their match in Bordeaux at France '98.

Like most people lucky enough to get a ticket, though, I was happy just being there to see the Socceroos, rollicking chants or otherwise. It had been 32 years almost to the day since an Australian team had last been at a World Cup. That game was in Hamburg, on 14 June 1974, when the Socceroos had held out for an hour against East Germany before defender Col Curran conceded an unlucky own goal and the aptly named Joachim Streich made it two ten minutes later. Of that Australia squad only Manfred Schaefer and Jack Reilly had made it back for the reprise three decades on, although I'd seen Jim Scane, the original Socceroos superfan and impromptu mascot of the '74 campaign, being wheeled onto a plane before I'd left Sydney. The *Sydney Morning Herald*'s John Huxley had written a piece about the 90-year-old missing out on the World Cup, and Emirates, apropos of nothing, had come in with free flights, accommodation and tickets for him and his grandson. It was a generous and selfless gesture, especially as the airline had the grace not to blow their own trumpet about it.

The drama of the win in Sydney and Australia's long hiatus from World Cup action meant expectations were high that the Socceroos would be firing the moment they took to the park, but whether it was big-stage jitters or a knock-on effect from Rotterdam, Australia had all the zip of a group of retirees in gumboots. Even before the still-disputed opening goal, when an out-of-position Mark Schwarzer collided with Atsushi Yanagisawa and was then knocked over by another Japanese player, the Socceroos appeared dazed, their sporadic incursions upfield failing to deliver genuine chances and losing shape immediately when the counterattack came. Were their brains being fried in the heat?

It seemed Hiddink's was. Or perhaps he was starting to

believe his own hype. How else to explain Luke Wilkshire's reappearance in the side? The underplayed Bristol City midfielder had been awful in the time he'd managed to stay on the pitch at De Kuip, yet here he was at right back, a position to which he was unaccustomed, with Brett Emerton pushed up into midfield. It was admirable of Hiddink to show faith in Wilkshire; he deserved another chance, but why give it to him now, in our most important game in 32 years?

In reality it had less to do with stubbornness and more to do with the fact that because of his youth and fitness Wilkshire was a player that Hiddink could utilise in all sorts of positions on the field while his older team-mates were still trying to catch their breath. In *Brilliant Orange*, Ruud Krol, a former Ajax Amsterdam and Holland player, explained that the so-called 'total football' system was as much a way of conserving energy as it was about players switching places.

'Our system was also a solution to a physical problem,' he said. 'Fitness has to be 100 per cent, but how can you play for 90 minutes and remain strong? If I, as left-back, run 70 metres up the wing, it's not good if I immediately have to run back 70 metres to my starting position. So, if the left-midfield player takes my place, and the left-winger takes the midfield position, then it shortens the distances. If you have to run ten times 70 metres and the same distance back ten times, that's a total of 1400 metres. If you change it so you must only run 1000 metres, you will be 400 metres fresher. That was the philosophy.'

Graham Arnold later confided there was simply no way Hiddink could countenance having Harry Kewell, Mark Bresciano and Tim Cahill on the field at the same time. Along with Mark Viduka, as a collective they were deemed too pregnable for opposition attacks and so put too much pressure on holding midfielder Vince Grella and the defenders behind him. The chief beneficiaries of this new dictum were the whippets of the team: Jason Culina, Brett Emerton and Luke Wilkshire. The chief victims, plainly, were the veterans: Stan Lazaridis, Josip Skoko and

Archie Thompson. None would see any game time during the tournament.

'Guus felt from what he'd seen at the Confederations Cup that defensively we weren't good enough,' Arnold said. 'We needed to have players on the field who would chase and chase and have a high work rate. Guus looks at athletes first and foremost. If a player basically can't get around the field as quick, well, he's pretty much pushed away out of his mind. Guus likes players who are very mobile, very adaptable, can play in more than one position, very athletic.'

Vim and vigour, though, can't always compensate for lack of skill. Within just three minutes of the start, Wilkshire was lucky to escape a yellow card after a late challenge on the Japanese defender Alessandro Santos, and would go on to be outwitted and outrun by the same player. Emerton would prove similarly ineffective, once falling over the ball with no one around him on the halfway line, and preferring to lob long passes crossfield when taking the ball to the byline might have been more damaging. The Blackburn Rovers player was quick, but didn't have the nous to convert forward motion into scoring opportunities. Each time he came within cooee of the goal he'd clumsily hand back the momentum to Zico's men.

'Emerton's a player exactly like Robbie Slater used to be,' Craig Foster told me. 'Emerton is better on the ball than Slater, but Slater was powerful, he'd donk it, use his speed and get in great crosses. But when he got anywhere near the goal, he'd put the ball out of the stadium.'

Good teams can carry one average performer, but on this day Australia as a unit weren't on their game. Slack passing, average marking and an overreliance on long balls from the back were putting unnecessary pressure on everyone and testing the nerves of the fans. Only rare moments of brilliance and industry from Viduka, Bresciano, Scott Chipperfield and a three-quarters-fit Kewell were keeping the tie alive.

The tension continued to ratchet up after half-time.

Schwarzer came out of the box to head the ball straight into the path of Naohiro Takahara, and was saved only by the leg of Lucas Neill. On 75 minutes, Chipperfield was dispossessed on the halfway line by Takahara, who had the goalmouth tantalisingly open but crossed square to Yanagisawa, who popped it up to Schwarzer. Yuichi Komano, too, wasted a chance three minutes later.

With just ten minutes left on the clock, it seemed Australia's great adventure was already over. Hiddink had run out of options. The Socceroos had promised so much, fought hard for their territory, but there was no getting away from the gnawing feeling that they'd been shown up as pretenders by a team they'd expected to beat. The Australians were not letting the Japanese rest for a second, but even if they nabbed a late goal, a draw wasn't going to be enough now. They'd left it too late. Or so they thought.

In *Japanese Rules,* former Japan coach Dettmar Cramer explained what the samurai called *zanshin*. 'It looks good if you take a sweeping cut [with a sword] at someone, and then just turn your back. But the fallen victim might summon up his last morsel of strength, and come back at you. So after you've taken a sweeping cut, you must remain alert until he has taken his last breath. That is *zanshin.* Japanese soccer does not have that.'

Typing furiously and barely raising their eyes to look at what was happening on the field, the correspondents for Australia's dailies began finessing the doomsday dispatches they'd started writing even before half-time. Where was Hiddink's famous luck? He had a nickname in Holland—'Guus Geluk' or Lucky Guus. But the Aussies couldn't take a trick. Were we instead seeing 'He Stinks!', the inglorious nickname Korean fans had given him before his miracle run in 2002?

Then, almost on cue, it happened. Eight minutes of mayhem. The sort of eight minutes a football fan would be happy to have once in a lifetime. In the centre of it all was one man, Tim Cahill, a player who just years before couldn't even get a game for Australia. The son of an English father and a Samoan mother, he'd been persuaded to turn out for a Western Samoa under-20 side as a substitute when he was 14, playing just a handful of minutes. That was enough for FIFA to declare he'd never represent Australia, the country of his birth, the country he'd grown up in, scampering around the suburban fields of Sydney. For close to a decade he'd fought for the right to wear the green and gold, even threatening to go to court. He'd been on the scrapheap. One of those what-if players, like Craig Johnston, Tony Dorigo and Josip Šimunić, who could have played for Australia but didn't. Then it all changed. A policy backflip. An FA Cup goal. A contract with Everton. A call-up against South Africa. When Cahill ran onto the field in the 53rd minute to replace Bresciano, he was still riding a wave that he didn't want to get off.

Now, there were just six minutes of normal time left on the clock. A long throw-in. A scuffed shot. A scramble in the area. *Goal.* Cahill ran to the left corner flag, sucked the screams of 20 million Aussies into his cheeks and shadow-boxed like a champion whipping up the crowd before a title fight. He didn't overdo the celebration. He knew the battle had only just begun.

A kid who'd come up through Millwall, the toughest club in England, with five reds and 70-odd yellows in his club career, Cahill had never been afraid to ride his luck. He returned down the ground and almost instantaneously chopped down Komano on the edge of the box after the winger had jinked in off the goal line. It was a foul. But Essam Abdel Fatah, the harried Egyptian ref, was probably still trying to figure out if he'd been right awarding the first goal to make a decision. Minutes later, Takashi Fukunishi was played into space by Shinji Ono. He steamed into the box, sidestepped Neill and let rip. The ball missed the inside netting by inches. Now there were just 60 seconds left. The play returned to the Australian half. John Aloisi, on for Wilkshire, collected the ball on the edge of the box, and laid it up square. Cahill was there. He tapped the ball forward with the bottom of his heel and swung his leg back like a golfer chipping onto the lip of a green. *Goal.* Australia had the lead for the first time in the match. Now it was Japan that had run out of time.

The third from Aloisi, a left-footed, defender-boondoggling slalom, was just too much for Japan to process. What had they done to deserve such misery? What had *we* done to deserve such fortune?

Goal. Goal. Goal. 3-1 to Australia. Zico dipped his head. Three points, *his* three points, had been stolen from him by a team he hadn't rated at all. When the whistle blew, the sound of DELETE keys being tapped frenetically on journalists' laptops was only drowned out by the cheering.

'Kokoda,' Jamo said to me ten minutes later, still shaking his head in wonder as we walked down to the press conference. 'We're over the Owen Stanley Ranges and Port Moresby's in view.'

Fortune favours the brave. The man who'd dropped Harry Kewell in Sydney strode imperiously into the poorly airconditioned press conference room, taking swigs from his bottle of water and smoothing down his hair. His face was red. His soiled shirt clung to his gut. Guus Geluk had saved the day.

'I don't think it's an escape,' he said, his charming Dutch-English filling the room. 'Escape is something when you get crucified by you [the media], in general. You can force your luck. If you sit back and you don't have a plan to see how the game can develop beforehand and you get your ball in, then it's luck. But when there's a plan then I can be very proud of the guys that they executed and practised on this and then it's nice to see that you pushed the luck.'

Hiddink wasn't very convincing—he *had* been lucky, and his substitutions had been reasonably straightforward given the desperate circumstances, not, as many were saying, the work of 'genius'. Ruud Gullit, the former Holland player and coach, said Hiddink had a 'horseshoe as big as my house'. But one Korean fan, Heejoon Park, blogging on the *Herald Sun* website after the game, put it down to something else altogether. He was convinced he'd seen the Dutchman perform 'a magic'.

'We Koreans are huge fans for Mr Hiddink,' Park wrote. 'When you were having been dominated by Japan until the half of the second half, I saw Hiddink on the TV, and I said to him in my mind, "Mr Hiddink, it's time to show us a magic." And wow! He really did it.'

You can't argue with the supernatural.

Arnold, though, insisted his boss had prepared the team to deal with any eventuality.

'The cue was that when Craig Moore came off and Josh Kennedy went on, that's when everyone knew what their jobs would be,' he said. 'Harry went from the middle out to the left-hand side, Emerton came back as a right-stopper, so then we had three quick guys at the back to counteract the counterattack, then we'd get the ball out to Emmo just over halfway, Johnny, Viduka and Josh would be in the middle, and Timmy would be around them. We felt, as well, that we could have started that way in the game—looking enough at Japan and seeing how they were defensively against high balls into the box. But if that backfires on us, what do we then revert to? So this was an option we tried to keep right up our sleeve until the end. It was something we fell back on to in case of need.'

'Guus knows how to tackle *every* situation,' confirmed Viduka, 'whether we're winning, losing or whatever. If you're clear in your mind on what you have to do in every situation, it makes the job a whole lot easier. As a bunch of guys, we know what to do in every situation.'

What Australia would have to do in their next game, against Brazil's *Titulares,* the anointed XI, had been equally thought out and analysed. But all the planning in the world would count for nothing if they didn't have the inner belief they could win it and the ability to make it happen. That, however, was not going to be a problem. After what had happened in Kaiserslautern, the Socceroos had it in spades.

Down on the Bremerstrasse, a drab thoroughfare by the rail line, Australian and Japanese fans were streaming into town an hour after the game. It was overwhelming to see how dedicated the fans were. Even at the Uruguay match in Sydney, there'd been thousands of supporters dressed in Wallabies or Kangaroos jerseys, which suggested that football hadn't fully arrived in our country just yet. In Kaiserslautern, though, almost every fan wore an official replica top, either generic or one with their favourite player's name emblazoned on the back. In years past, the only name you would have expected to see, if you'd been so lucky to even *find* a Socceroos jersey in a store, was KEWELL. Now there was BRESCIANO. POPOVIC. GRELLA. SKOKO. All good Aussie names.

At one point, a bloke in a kangaroo costume, tired of seeing the crowd held up every couple of minutes by a black FIFA limousine, ran into the middle of the road and tried to direct traffic himself. The *polizei,* in their khaki shirts and green berets, had a laugh and with a minimum of fuss moved him on. When he'd been shifted the required few metres, the kangaroo took a call on his mobile. It was the surreal highlight of a surreal day in Germany.

That night, back in Strasbourg, former France international Christian Karembeu, a World Cup winner, wore a Socceroos shirt while being interviewed on television. I had no idea what he was saying, but when he pinched the front of his shirt to show the TV audience, his body language said he was wearing it with pride. In the Socceroos he'd obviously seen something he liked.

France was yet to play their first game—that was the next day, against Switzerland—so the bars were going about their normal business. It was almost ten o'clock, but the sun had only just gone down. Place Kléber was teeming with young lovers and groups of teenagers who were oblivious to what had just taken place barely 150 kilometres away.

I left the apartment and found Jamo and Harro, unwashed and still in their Socceroos T-shirts, in a bistro that was showing the end of the Italy vs Ghana game, 'ALLEMAGNE 2006—LA COUPE DU MONDE DE FOOTBALL!—COMME SI VOUS Y ÉTIEZ!' said the flyer in the window. It wasn't quite just like being there, but the atmosphere was convivial. The owner, a small fat man in his forties, was too busy taking orders and wiping down tables to take any notice of what was happening on the flat-screen TV bolted to the wall. I ordered a plate of tortellini and a beer and settled in for the rest of the game.

With 15 minutes left on the clock, the Ghanaians were desperate for an equaliser to Italy's first-half goal and had the most irrepressible midfield I'd seen all tournament. But as with Australia's build-up play for 80 minutes in Kaiserslautern, the Africans couldn't convert. Italy were doing the bare minimum to hold on to their lead. I was rooting for Ghana—I wanted an African team to do well—but there was an air of inevitability about the result. There always is when the Italians play.

This night would be no exception. Sammy Kuffour mistimed a back pass after collecting an Andrea Pirlo lob from midfield, substitute Vincenzo Iaquinta intercepted, stepped around the goalkeeper and poked a low shot into an open goal to make it 2-0. He ran to the left post, arms outstretched, mouth agape, and collapsed on his back to be buried under his team-mates. We drained our drinks. The World Cup had seen enough fairytales for one day.

On my first trip to Germany, I'd stood in a street just off the medieval Romerberg Square in Frankfurt and asked my guide, a bird-faced young woman with a Leo Sayer perm, why there weren't any monuments to the German war dead. Everywhere I'd been during my ten-day journey through southern Germany and the Rhineland I had been inundated with information about the civic authorities' great shame about the country's Nazi past. This shame was physically and appropriately embodied in all manner of monuments, sculptures and plaques to the genocide victims. But there was nothing to commemorate the estimated two million Germans who had been killed, and the 12 million displaced, mostly in the east, after the end of the war.

'It is not something we do,' she replied, looking faintly embarrassed. It was something she didn't want to talk about either. She turned on her heel and walked a few hundred metres down the street to the next 'attraction'.

However, my guide wasn't telling the whole truth. Germany's new chancellor, Angela Merkel, had come into the job supporting the concept of a Centre for Expulsions in Berlin, a facility that would document this secret history of the forced removal of ethnic Germans and other nationalities from eastern Europe after the Third Reich's collapse. The Berlin project, and the 2006 World Cup, were important to Germany because they were loud statements to the world that it had finally decided to move on from half a century of guilt.

The Germans have a typically unpronounceable word for coming to terms with their history, *Vergangenheitsbewältigung*, or 'wrestling down the past'. For most of the postwar period, they achieved it by living in denial. From the 1970s onwards, they achieved it by introducing draconian laws outlawing such acts as displaying swastikas or giving Nazi salutes. Even today, with the world riven by terrorism and regional violence, there is still a reluctance to deploy the German national army because of its Nazi history, even though Italy and Japan—two equally guilty parties in the wartime fascist trident—are not held up to quite the same scrutiny.

Germany 2006, though, was to change all the rules about how Germans should behave. Freed by football from their prison of shame, the flag was flying everywhere. Kids were comfortable painting their faces in black, red and gold. The national anthem was sung with gusto. As Beckenbauer had wanted, his people were allowing themselves to crack a smile. They were even feeling *good*.

In the national football team especially, the change was plain to see. The dour, stolid, defensive but effective style that had so characterised *Nationalmannschaft* sides of the past had been replaced by a new emphasis on attack, fitness and flair. Klinsmann's boys had opened the Cup in Munich on 9 June with a 4-2 win over Costa Rica. No one had seriously expected the hosts to lose to the Central Americans, but it was the aggressive manner of the victory, and the sheer number of goals collected, that suggested a very different Germany. As 'Klinzi' had said before the World Cup, his team's brief was not just to win the tournament but to exploit 'the opportunity to show the world who we are'. His country had the 'possibility to redefine Germany: to create a brand'.

If youth and optimism were driving Germany into a new era, France was running on an altogether different motor, one that threatened to clap out long before the final on 9 July. It had been eight years since *Les Bleus* had humiliated Brazil 3-0 in the Stade de France—by no means an eternity. But it had also been eight years since they had scored a goal in a World Cup match, that same night in Paris, which *was* an eternity. And where Klinsmann was young and hip—as hip as one can be with a bleached mullet in your recent past—new French coach Raymond Domenech was old and cerebral, affecting a professorial look that might have won him adorers on a lectern at the Sorbonne but looked decidedly out of place in the team dugout. A former defensive midfielder with Olympique Lyonnais and long-time coach of the French youth team, Domenech had unusual methods which, according to legend, included making Zinedine Zidane and three team-mates attend a performance of Samuel Beckett's *Endgame* before an important match. Whether this had anything to do with the retirement of Zidane, Lilian Thuram and Claude Makelele a month after

Domenech took the job is unclear. (Perhaps they might have stayed had he bought a few bags of popcorn and hired a DVD of *Gladiator* instead, like football coaches everywhere.)

Football was no longer the social glue it had been eight years before, when Jacquet's licorice all-sorts team silenced far-right leader Jean-Marie Le Pen. After the September 11 attacks, the sense of shared identity between black, white and *beur* (French-born but of North African origin) had evaporated. Even Le Pen was blustering again, telling the French sports daily *L'Equipe* later in the tournament: 'France doesn't totally recognise itself in this team. Maybe the coach exaggerated the proportion of players of colour, maybe in this area he should have been a bit more careful, maybe he got carried away in his ideology.'

Politicians and sociologists didn't have any answers for France's woes. But if their football team could win the World Cup, everything about *La Republique* would be right again. Yet their results in qualifying were mediocre. A depleted *Les Bleus* had drawn with Israel in September 2004, drew with the Republic of Ireland a month later, and then drew again with Switzerland in March 2005. They hadn't put a goal away in 270 minutes. But when Zidane, Thuram and Makelele reversed their retirements en masse, this triggered an immediate turn-around in form that would see France ultimately top its group. Amazingly, it was France's first successful World Cup qualifying campaign since 1986, having automatically qualified as hosts in '98. A shock loss to Slovakia at home in March—their first in 18 games—rightly sounded alarm bells again, but subsequent victories over Mexico, Denmark and China showed the old stagers, whom *Le Parisien* newspaper had cleverly likened to 'the Rolling Stones on their farewell tour', still had the requisite swagger. Like the Stones, unfortunately, their best days were also well behind them.

That was immediately apparent in France's opening game against Switzerland on 13 June. I watched it with Jamo and Harro in a bar off Place Kléber, in a room full of young Algerian and Tunisian students. Thierry Henry, the most feared striker in world football, barely got a chance the whole 90 minutes, the best attack taking place when Zidane gave his team-mates William Gallas and Sylvain Wiltord a spray on the sideline. Down the other end, it was little better. The geriatric Fabien Barthez was fortunate to escape with a clean sheet, faffing about in goal and regularly getting himself out of position.

It was easily the worst game of the tournament so far, enlivened only by the presence of a young French footballer called Franck Ribery, who was quick, tenacious and had the most unusual face, courtesy of it going through a windshield when he was two. He was a Muslim who had been anointed as Zidane's successor but, because this was only his debut, was a long way from establishing a Zidane-like authority among his team-mates. A bitchy Henry put him in his place in the press conference afterwards.

'Franck placed the ball behind me instead of placing it in front of me,' he said. 'If he had placed it in front of me I could have pushed it inside an empty goal without controlling it and that would have been a goal. He is young and it was not easy for him. He brought us what he could and *some* of it was good.'

When we left the bar, it was almost 9 pm yet the sun was still high in the sky, making it feel like late afternoon. Preparations were being made for *le grand depart,* the start of the Tour de France. Landscapers had moved in, constructing garden beds and positioning huge outsized terracotta pots. Sprinklers had been installed to help the turf and flowers survive the heat, and young girls and boys were spraying their faces in the billows of mist. We strolled over to the tomb of General Kléber, killing time before Brazil's opener against Croatia in Munich, a game that would answer a lot of questions about Australia's likely fate in Germany.

Already this World Cup was subverting all the scripts. Australia had run over the top of Japan. Ecuador had thumped Poland, Trinidad & Tobago had kept Sweden to a scoreless draw.

The mighty France, it appeared, was gone already. Germany was flying high. General Kléber, however, standing before us in bronze, his skeleton under our feet, proved that sometimes things don't always turn out the way you think.

CHAPTER FOUR · CIRCUS MAXIMUS

'Futebol é uma caixinha de surpresas.'
('Football is a little box of surprises.')

BRAZILIAN SAYING

John Aloisi's day job was in Vittoria, northern Spain, for a club called Deportivo Alavés in the Spanish second division. As the only Australian to have played in the world's top football league (he'd been transferred from Primera Liga outfit Osasuna the previous season), he understood better than most how it felt to be regarded as an oddity from the Antipodes. The Spanish knew very little, if anything, about Australians, he told me, and their general knowledge of Australian culture and lifestyle was so poor 'some people think we have kangaroos as pets'.

'People over here don't really know much about Australian soccer,' he said. 'They don't know any players that play in our national team. They only really know me as the "Australian player" and they think the national team is me and players who've never left Australia.'

The Socceroos might have stunned the critics with their win in Kaiserslautern, but searching for Australia merchandise—a jersey, a stuffed kangaroo, even a measly flag—in the shops along Strasbourg's Rue des Grandes Arcades was, like Aloisi's experience in Navarra, somewhat of a comedown. The few World Cup displays consisted of copious Zidane merchandise and a smattering of French jerseys, or the distinctive shirts of Brazil, Portugal and Spain. Australian football wasn't on

Europe's sporting radar at all; in fact, it was hard to find anything Australian anywhere.

The phenomenon of Australian footballers in Europe is a misnomer, if you count England as distinct from the continent. Most players who've left home since Joe Marston stumped up at Preston North End in 1950 have, for reasons of opportunity and cultural affinity, chosen the British Isles as their proving ground. Australian footballers in the continent's big leagues are a rarer breed. Rarer still are those who become stars, names that European kids look up to and try to emulate. Before Mark Bresciano became Australia's first ever $20 million-plus footballer at Parma in Italy, Robbie Slater—at Racing Club de Lens in northern France—was probably our closest thing to a bona fide celebrity in continental football. Others have made big impressions in lesser leagues—Paul Okon, Frank Farina and Eddie Krncevic in Belgium, Mark Viduka in Croatia—but very few Australians have graduated to the big time of the English, Italian and Spanish premier divisions. Hence our national team has remained a curiosity, a bunch of unknowns. An understandable state of affairs if you appreciate that before Australia's game against Germany at the 2005 Confederations Cup, a full-strength Australia side had not played on the continent for five years, its last outing a 3-0 drubbing of Hungary in Budapest in 2000.

Yet just an hour and a half's drive north-east of Strasbourg, one town was getting to know quite a lot about our national team. The Socceroos and its caravan of supporters and media had been holed up there for over a week. The only pet kangaroos spotted had been inflatable ones, carried around the necks of fans as they took in team training or paraded through the streets.

Outside the newly relaid Otto-Meister Stadion, the home of TSG Öhringen and the temporary training ground for the Socceroos, hundreds of fans had gathered on a grassy knoll behind a tall wire fence. Some had their faces pressed up against the mesh. A few were standing back a bit, trying to get long-distance snaps of their heroes. Others, bored with seeing nothing, had started a scratch game.

The players could have been excused for not paying much attention to them. Quite apart from trying to impress Guus Hiddink, Johan Neeskens, Graham Arnold and the team's retinue of trainers with their limited opportunities, they were a good 200 metres from the fence, separated by an athletics circuit and a platoon of security goons. Europe's heatwave had not spared Öhringen. The only shade on offer was under the main stand, and that was for the media and some fortunate local schoolkids. No wonder the fans were screaming at the top of their lungs to get noticed. The players had to squint into the glare of the midday sun to even guess they were there.

I joined the throng at the fence for a minute or two, but found the squad was so far away it wasn't worth the effort. So I got inside the media entrance where at least I could walk onto the pitch and see the faces of the players. Behind the running track, the usual suspects were struggling to keep out of the sun: Fairfax's Michael Cockerill was chatting to John Kosmina; Matthew Hall was complaining about bandwagons; his wife, Anita, was talking to a group of student filmmakers from Hamburg who were making a documentary about the Socceroos' time in Öhringen. Peter Wilkins, sweltering inside a grey suit, was pacing up and down the sideline. Ray Martin, an odd sight at a football ground, was scribbling on a notepad. The gossip was that the FFA had relaxed its strict media rules so that Martin could interview the players for puff pieces for *60 Minutes*.

I didn't see what point was being served keeping the fans penned in. They'd come from the other end of the world to cheer on their team and were being treated like sheep in a holding yard. They deserved better. But football was a whole different ball game now. Hiddink was keeping the team on a tight leash. When the Australians had first arrived in town, they'd snubbed an official civic reception at the town hall—brass bands, little kids, Öhringen's hoi polloi—sending Luke Wilkshire and three wide-eyed development players instead of the full squad.

On this day, though, Tim Cahill walked over and did his best to acknowledge the fans. He picked up an Adidas +Teamgeist ball and punted it over the fence into the crowd. Scrapping wildly, grown men fought over it like seagulls tearing apart a packet of fish and chips.

At the 'G'day Mate' festival in the town's main square, the atmosphere was more inclusive. Green and gold vinyl tablecloths had been set on foldaway tables and Aussie beer was flowing. Local teenage boys and girls performed bizarre choreography to techno music while dressed in the kits of some of the competing nations. Older townsfolk paraded in the traditional dress of the area and happily posed for photographs. John O'Neill, on behalf of the again conspicuously absent Socceroos, gamely sang 'Waltzing Matilda' to a generous cheer.

To escape the sun, I wandered down a side alley and found an outside table at a pub. The ponytailed André Krüger walked up and stopped briefly for a chat. Krüger has the odd celebrity of being the Socceroos' greatest fan, even though he's spent his entire life in Germany. He became interested in Australia as a child in Hanover, and by the time the Socceroos rocked up to the 1974 World Cup he was obsessed. Krüger was now a folk hero to a lot of supporters and, with the Socceroos making their heroic return to a World Cup on his own turf, he was revelling in the attention. (He was hardly incognito—he had KRUEGER on the back of his Aussie jersey.) As we got talking, I noticed he had an old bloke with him who was wearing a Socceroos shirt and baseball cap, had dyed brown hair and looked about 70. It was Ted Smith, who'd played two games for Australia at the 1956 Melbourne Olympics. When Krüger got waylaid by some autograph seekers, I introduced myself. Smith gently touched my shoulder and leaned in. I asked him how he was feeling.

'I'm walking on cloud nine,' he said, his eyes glistening. 'I never thought I'd see the day. I missed out on a World Cup as a player, and I always thought I would as a fan, but I'm here now. There's Australians here from everywhere. Germany's beautiful. *Beautiful.*"

And with those words, my cynicism about the antics at the training ground and the no-show Socceroos and everything else I'd seen and heard so far in Öhringen disappeared.

Three weeks out from the start of Germany 2006, while the world was devouring profiles of the two Ronaldos and betting agencies were installing Brazil as unbackable favourites to win a sixth World Cup, a civil war was raging in Brazil's biggest city, São Paulo. The few images coming out of the country were cinematic in their rawness and violence. Gangsters from the Primeiro Comando da Capital (First Command of the Capital), a ruthless crime syndicate, had mounted coordinated terrorist attacks inside 80 prisons and on the streets in protest over the relocation of hundreds of its members to a remote penal facility. Police and fire stations were bombed, vehicles torched, hundreds of civilians slaughtered. The four days of carnage only ended when the gang's kingpin, Marcos Willians Herbas Camacho, aka 'Marcola', called for his foot soldiers to release their hostages. In return for their compliance, Marcola had a simple request: new plasma TVs for his men to watch the World Cup.

So in a country where even civil wars come to a halt for football, to earn the yellow shirt of the national football team marks a player as exceptional. It's when 11 of those players come together that the real trouble begins. The boys from Brazil have forever grappled with the curse of overconfidence, what they call *oba oba.* The better the *Seleção,* the more crippling *oba oba* becomes. The curse struck instantly at the 1966 World Cup in England after Brazil had won the previous two tournaments in a canter. The 1982 team, regarded by some experts as the best Brazilian side ever assembled, didn't get past the quarters in Spain, eliminated by eventual winners Italy 3-2 in Barcelona.

In Germany, the spectre of *oba oba* was bigger than ever. With a line-up containing Ronaldinho, Kaká, Adriano, Ronaldo, Robinho and Roberto Carlos, among others, and a World Cup-winning coach in Carlos Alberto Parreira, there could be no excuses. How could there be? Failure was not an option—it never had been in Brazilian football. Dida, the team's number one, had spent the previous months begging his country to forgive the 'crucified' figure of the late and unlamented Moacir Barbosa, the goalkeeper who'd had the grave misfortune of letting in Uruguay's winning goal in the World Cup final ... *in 1950.*

Brazilian players and management, though, appeared oblivious to the dark presence stalking them. Before the tournament, they'd arranged little more than training runs against a Fluminense under-20 side, a Lucerne invitational XI and New Zealand, banging in 25 unanswered goals; their only serious friendly, against Russia in Moscow, had been played in the middle of the Russian winter, in temperatures approaching -30°C. Hardly ideal preparation for a balmy German summer.

They'd been paid millions just to train. The small city of Weggis in Switzerland had stumped up US$2 million and thrown in free accommodation in a five-star hotel. Their training sessions were promoted like rock concerts, tickets being sold for €17 and snapped up in seconds. No one within the squad seemed to have their heads screwed on right—the players had asked to do away with shared accommodation and demanded individual rooms. Strikers Ronaldo and Adriano, the two players who looked most out of shape and needed to knuckle down, partied hard on their days off. Arrogantly, Parreira was already talking about meeting Germany in the final.

Ronaldo, Golden Boot winner at Korea-Japan 2002, was under considerable pressure going into the Australia game, after an opening performance against Croatia in which he appeared to do nothing at all. One Brazilian journalist even refused to give him a rating out of ten, so lackadaisical and inconsequential had his contribution been. His substitute and

Real Madrid team-mate Robinho had, in sharp contrast, been energetic and impressive. But first performances historically don't count for much; Brazil had been slow starters in all their World Cups and took some time to get their groove. Indeed, most of the first XI had been off their game in Berlin, only Kaká's skills matching the wattage produced by the flashes of the fans' cameras. Certainly Parreira's unstinting faith in Ronaldo was stretching credulity, just as the player's official weight for the Australia game: 82 kg. He'd arrived in Switzerland at 95 kg, and had lost three or four kilograms at the most. Brazil's tight-fitting dri-fit tops couldn't lie. *O Fendômeno* had become *O Fatômeno.* The suspicion that Parreira was keeping him in the team just so Ronaldo could break Just Fontaine's goalscoring record was hard to shake.

The Socceroos, however, wouldn't be fooled. They knew it would take an extraordinary effort to come away with a result in Munich, with or without Ronaldo. The key to an improbable victory wasn't technical ability but mindset. Lucas Neill, the most headstrong of the Australian players, wasn't buying into the David-versus-Goliath talk about the match.

'If you worry too much about your opponent, then you take away the strength of your own game,' he told me. 'We're an unpredictable team and we're a very good team. If we play to all our strengths, hopefully that will cancel out what everybody else is trying to do. Maybe Brazil will find themselves defending more than attacking.'

The New Yorker's architecture critic Paul Goldberger had called Allianz Arena a 'quilted doughnut'. Locals called it the *Schlauchboot,* the 'Inflatable Boat'. To me it looked like a girl's elastic hairband. Whatever it was supposed to be, it was hard to miss coming down the A99 from Stuttgart. Made from ETFE or ethylene tetra fluoro ethylene, a high-tech plastic, it was renowned for glowing blue or red to denote whatever local Bundesliga team was playing there on any given day: red for Bayern Munich, blue for 1860 Munich, and sometimes red and blue just for the hell of it.

On 18 June 2006, at noon, on a killer summer's day, it was white. I had hoped the World Cup organisers might have switched on some yellow or green lights—which would have been neutral, after all—but it hadn't happened. Instead, the concrete ramps and car parks outside the stadium were flowing with two shades of yellow: the lime of Brazil and the banana of Australia. It was hard to tell them apart. It was also something the world would probably never see again. Getting a full-strength Brazil to come to Australia was a pipedream. The last time they had travelled west over the Pacific, in 1999, when Soccer Australia was arranging matches with club sides, the Confederação Brasileira de Futebol had sent an under-23 team. Ronaldo and Harry Kewell, the star attractions for the fans, hadn't bothered to turn up. Today, they were both playing, Ronaldo—on the basis of his poor form—possibly for the last time. Neither team could meet later in this World Cup.

Chatting with the fans outside the stadium, though, I soon discovered all the talk was not of history being made but of Sam Newman's assault of a Fanatic at the 'Samba Party' at the Löwenbräukeller Beer Hall the night before. The fan, later identified as airline steward Anthony Demovic, had called the Melbourne TV identity a 'poofter in a pink shirt' and spat on him. It was hard to know what was more galling: the punch-up, the spitting or the fact that Newman was in Munich. I'd had no idea *The Footy Show* was even in Germany to film a special, nor that Peter FitzSimons had been flown out by Channel Nine for the program. Shane Warne, Eddie McGuire, Paul Vautin and Garry Lyon were questionable enough comperes for a show about football, but FitzSimons? It was like Monica Lewinsky doing an ad for breath mints. If it was an attempt by Nine to steal some ratings, it didn't work. If it was an attempt to connect with football fans, it failed abysmally. The only thing it accomplished was to highlight again how out of touch the station was with a sport it had never come to grips with. But some good would come out of the whole sorry episode. Johnny Warren could at least rest in peace knowing FitzSimons had finally answered his own question, 'What World Cup?'

Australian sport has had its great moments of theatre—Jack Johnson circling Tommy Burns like a panther in Sydney Stadium in 1908, Gary Ablett fighting a one-man war against Hawthorn at the MCG in 1989, Wally Lewis going nose to nose with Mark Geyer at Lang Park in 1991, Cathy Freeman in the Olympic Stadium in 2000. The frisson of excitement around the stands of Allianz Arena heightened the feeling that Australians were about to witness a similar moment for the ages. The reserves doing their drills. The high mesh fences behind the goals. The Bob Sinclar music. The roar of a whole stand of fans as a Mexican wave passed through. Goleo the lion dancing for the cameras. The VIPs. The drums. The hundreds of millions of people watching. Germany's Circus Maximus demanded something special. Yet the Socceroos weren't overawed by the occasion. In fact, they took to the pitch with nothing to lose. Just before 6 pm, news had filtered in of Japan's goalless draw with Croatia in Nuremburg, eliminating the spectre of goal ratio from Australia's pre-game planning. A win or draw would now see the Socceroos qualify for the second round. A loss would mean that the game everyone expected to be the crunch clash of Group F, against Croatia, would be just that. Australia could run onto the field and just play.

By quirk of fate, I took my seat almost directly behind Hiddink and the Australian bench. A gum-chewing Arnold was nervously pacing the sideline, enjoying some banter with fans. Hiddink seemed deep in thought, holding his chin in the crook of his thumb. A few metres away was Parreira, the legendary Mario Zagallo, and the Brazilian bench.

The opening minutes followed a fairly predictable pattern: the *Seleção* building up their attack with short, carefully measured passes. Australia, a step off the pace, conceded a free kick to Kaká within the first two minutes but Ronaldinho's lame effort was cleared away by Mark Viduka downfield. Then Brazil showed what it could do in the blink of an eye. Roberto Carlos punted the ball back down the left flank, it bounced once and found Lucio, who was dispossessed by Craig Moore. Only Moore's miskick ended up in the path of Kaká, who headed on to Ronaldo. The heavyweight striker received it cleanly on his chest, then volleyed over his head to where Kaká, now steaming in directly behind him, smacked it hard into the advertising hoarding behind the left goalpost. Mark Schwarzer, who'd barely had time to spit on his gloves, was sent rolling on the grass.

'The spirit of Australia is the flying kangaroo, mate,' Viduka had laughed when we spoke before the tournament. 'We've gotta fly at 'em. We've gotta take 'em on. It would be a shame if we tried to play "bunker system" or something like that. It wouldn't utilise what kind of players we have. Going forward we've got so many good players. My philosophy is attack is the best defence.'

It was a wonderful sentiment, and that's all it might have stayed. But, true to the captain's word, the Australians immediately hit back, Viduka himself unleashing an in-swinging strike that came off his boot at half pace. Neill then made a terrific run through midfield, beating Zé Roberto, but was foiled by Lúcio. On seven minutes, Moore, falling to his feet after a back pass from Jason Culina, kicked a 30-metre cutout pass to Scott Chipperfield who sent Mile Sterjovski scuttling through to the byline. There were signs of life in this team. Brett Emerton was containing Ronaldinho. Chipperfield was outfoxing Cafu. A pumped-up Vince Grella was tormenting anyone who came his way and was lucky not to be sent off for a studs-up tackle on Ronaldo.

Only their finishing, Australia's bête noire, was letting them down, Culina botching two corners, one long-range strike and a free kick. Still, the performance had been encouraging. Brazil had reverted to playing long balls for their strikers to get through the six-man midfield. Australia, in contrast, were pushing the ball around on the deck, keeping possession. 'GO AUSSIE! GO AUSSIE! GO AUSSIE!' reverberated around the stadium.

When Viduka drew Lúcio, Zé Roberto and Emerson and still managed to thread the ball to Culina, the PSV Eindhoven midfielder again wasted good lead-up work. Another chance was squandered when Chipperfield trundled down the left wing and played in Sterjovski near the corner flag, but Sterjovski let the ball run out of play on the referee's whistle. Except the ref, the German Markus Merk, hadn't blown; it had come from the crowd.

There were other moments of intrepid play. Emerton and Culina combined for a dazzling one-two down the left, fooling Zé Roberto, Ronaldinho and Roberto Carlos. Culina, atoning for his earlier profligacy, combined with Viduka to set up a rampaging Mark Bresciano, whose strike whistled over Dida's crossbar.

Brazil didn't know where to look. Ronaldinho, the most gifted player in the world, made his first real burst only on the 20-minute mark but was denied by Neill at the edge of the box. He was so rattled by the Aussies' marking, he later stepped on the ball when in a position to score. Ronaldo was also badly off the pace. He flailed theatrically in mid-air to ruin one scoring opportunity and his sole good strike from an Adriano backheel was blocked by Neill.

It had been a bravura show by the Socceroos, a performance that in just 45 minutes had exploded the myths about the Australian game—the resorting to thuggery, reliance on the long ball, lack of invention, poor tactical discipline. Whatever historical baggage Australia had taken into the World Cup had been unceremoniously dumped.

Emerton had banished all memories of his ordinary effort in Kaiserslautern to be arguably best on ground, Neill's presence in defence was omnipotent, and Viduka was in breathtaking form. Hiddink, by turns pensive or manic on the sideline, could no longer be suspected of quackery: he'd backed up after a shaky outing against Japan to demonstrate there really was some substance to the hype. Unleashing Bresciano just before half-time, just like his switch of Kewell for Popovic in Sydney, had given the team a new edge.

'Guus is able to get the best out of every individual,' Bresciano told me. 'Just the way he approaches the game, the way he talks, his motivational skills, his ability to read a game. He's not quiet and not over the top. He's got the right medicine. When he came in, everyone started from zero and that's why our intensity and our performance increased. Aussies don't muck around, mate. If we've got a job to do, we'll do it.'

So how to account for what happened just after the break? If anything, it proved that Ronaldo was still a force to be reckoned with, a player who might have been overweight and slow, but had the brains to think two or three movements ahead. The goal seemed too easy. It was made from a Ronaldinho straight pass from near the centre of the pitch to a fractionally offside Ronaldo on the left edge of the box. He drew Emerton, Neill and Moore and crossed square to Adriano, who had no trouble threading it through Chipperfield's legs. It was a bitterly disappointing goal to concede. More disappointing, though, was the failure to pull a goal when Australia had the world champions back-pedalling on the counterattack. The tension was immense. Arnold was gesticulating frantically on the sideline, trying to get Hiddink's tactical changes communicated to the players. 'BRESH! BRESH! COME HERE!' he screamed. Hiddink, also unusually agitated, was having hassles with the fourth official.

Viduka got the ball in the centre of the park, held off Zé Roberto, and nipped it past Emerson to Cahill, who put in Bresciano down the left flank. He had no one but Dida to beat, but paused to cut back in and was filched by Zé Roberto. Then a

Dida blunder gifted Kewell, who was on for Cahill, but he blew his shot in front of an open goal. Minutes later, he sweetly hit a long-range shot but it grazed the top of the crossbar. Stunned, the Brazilian fans began booing their own team. Who the hell were these colonial upstarts? Brazil's fans weren't used to seeing their national team scrambling back in defence, sortie upon sortie. The wrong team had the upper hand. This was the Hiddink effect in action. More than any other coach in the world, he knew when and how to deploy his substitutes. Now he was bringing on John Aloisi, one of the more competent finishers in his squad, to buttress an attack that was already running hot laps around the Brazilians.

Parreira, like an old man on the other side of a chessboard, had his own plan. On came Robinho for Ronaldo, Gilberto Silva for Emerson. With almost his first touch, Robinho danced around Chipperfield and unleashed a fierce strike past Schwarzer's left post. Minutes later, he forced the Australian goalkeeper to save off his legs. The intent was clear. Shut the Socceroos down. Knock 'em out. Except the Aussies' resolve was unshaken.

The action was end to end. Bresciano had a half-bicycle kick from an Aloisi header saved by Dida, and Viduka, under pressure, had a volley swallowed in the roof of the net. Downfield, Brazil's best chance came when a zipping header from Kaká hit the near post off a Ronaldinho corner. The Brazilians had been pushed back onto the ropes. It was a measure of how good the Australians were playing that the *Seleção* were relying on long aerial balls to mount any sort of effective offence.

But Parreira had one final trick up his sleeve. He pulled off Adriano and threw on Frederico Chaves Guedes, or Fred, the Olympique Lyonnais striker who had the enviable record of scoring the fastest goal in Brazilian football—3.17 seconds. It was the killer blow. It took just 108 seconds to open his World Cup account.

The FIFA official, an Engelbert Humperdinck lookalike, was amused. There we were, the international press, pinned up against a flimsy partition like cattle jostling for space in a slaughter yard, thrusting our voice recorders into the face of the greatest footballer on the planet, Ronaldinho. He might have had something interesting to say, except a) I couldn't get within two metres of him and b) he was speaking in Portuguese, a language for which I have no faculty whatsoever. Still, I pressed forward, desperate for a quote, any quote, beseeching Brazil's number ten to turn his boggle-eyed gaze my way. 'DINHO! AUSTRALIAN! AUSTRALIAN REPORTER!' If it were possible, the journalists behind me looked even more anguished. It must have been a pathetic sight, which explained Humperdinck's smirk. It was also futile. In seconds, Ronaldinho had been bundled ahead by his minders into the blazing lights of the waiting TV cameras.

I'd never seen a post-match press free-for-all like it. Five hundred journos—mostly Brazilian and Japanese—sweltering inside a space the size of a car showroom, with no airconditioning and a corridor for players and staff snaking through the middle of the maelstrom. The 'mixed zone' is what FIFA calls it, a term which suggests an air of peaceful fraternisation between players and press; in reality, it's little more than an uncivilised shitfight.

Most of the Australian players were happy to chat, though Cahill stormed right through. Perhaps he was still annoyed at having been subbed for Kewell. The Liverpool winger himself was keeping an equally low profile, perhaps mindful that anything he said could compromise his chances of escaping a ban for verbally abusing Merk after the match.

Culina, more diplomatically, thought 'individual brilliance' turned the game, but the 'referee could have done a little bit too'. Neill was typically downcast—he always is, given his natural competitiveness—and said 'if it wasn't for two dubious goals the game could have been a lot different', but admitted the Aussies hadn't made the most of their opportunities: 'At this level it's very hard to score goals ... it hurts badly because we created four or five good chances against the world champions; we had chances to score but we didn't take them.' Viduka continued in the same vein: 'We were hurting them ... in the first half we played some nice football, but we didn't get into the area where we could *really* hurt them.' Grella was asked how the Brazilians had reacted after the final whistle. What had they said to the Socceroos? 'Well done. Good luck. Same sort of bullshit everyone says after a game,' he said, wiping his chin and looking at the floor. 'Nothing special, mate, nothing special.'

Grella's honesty was charming but jolting. Life went on. It was over. No matter how valiantly they had played, or how amazing the experience had been, Brazil had still won and Australian football, after a short flight in orbit, had been brought crashing back to earth.

CHAPTER FIVE · RIPPING UP THE TABLECLOTHS

'In football everything is complicated by the presence of the other team.'

JEAN-PAUL SARTRE

Tito's Yugoslavia was once a powerhouse of European football, but the irresistible force of history had detonated communism in the early 1990s and split the national side into half a dozen new teams. Two of them, the strongest, were in Germany: Croatia and Serbia & Montenegro. In a bizarre turn of events, they became a trio for all intents and purposes, as Montenegrins had voted to secede from Belgrade three weeks before the tournament started.

A narrow loss for Serbia & Montenegro in its opening game against Holland had been followed by a catastrophic 6-0 humiliation by Argentina, and with those two defeats the most admired defence in Europe—the Serbs conceded just one goal in qualifying—had been reduced to a bickering, jaded mess. Amid the internecine strife, an Australian midfielder, Ivan Ergić, would start for the Balkan team in its third match, a dead rubber against Ivory Coast in Munich. So fluid is the concept of nationality in football that before the tournament kicked off, Ergić, ex-Perth Glory, had not yet played for Serbia, was born in Croatia and had an Australian passport.

His case wasn't exceptional—Tony Dorigo had turned out for England at Italia '90—but Germany 2006 was, given that three other Australians were selected for one foreign squad: Croatia.

These were typical Aussie boys who'd enjoyed typical

Aussie childhoods, been to typical Aussie schools, and had typical Aussie aspirations. They were Aussie through and through. Yet when Croatia came calling in 1997, that wasn't enough for Hajduk Split's Anthony Šerić to stay loyal. As far as he saw it (rightly or wrongly), Australia offered no viable path to the World Cup. Four years later, Hertha Berlin's Josip Šimunić followed. Joey Didulica, then of Austria Wien, made his switch in 2004 when it became clear he was behind Mark Schwarzer and Zeljko Kalac in the pecking order of goalkeepers for the Germany 2006 campaign.

The vilification of these men by some fans and parts of the local press was extreme. They were hardly doing anything that hadn't been done before, even by Australia, for whom newly arrived British and eastern European talent had formed the bulk of national squads in the 1970s and '80s. In this new era of ridiculous money and loose morals, loyalty to club was a quaint eccentricity; it was inevitable that loyalty to country would become just another thing to hock. For years, Italian, French and Spanish clubs had been doling out forged EU passports and other documents to South American players they couldn't bear to part with under foreign quota restrictions. There were five Brazilians playing for countries other than Brazil at this World Cup. This was the ugly reality of international football. Where there was money, there was opportunity. Where there was opportunity, there were pragmatic choices to make. Some people can make these choices and live with them. Šimunić, Šerić and Didulica had made theirs and never looked back.

If there were positives for Australia in their defections, it was that their opportunism made players such as Mark Viduka—who'd played in Croatia, owned property there and married a Croatian girl—more admirable. The same with Josip Skoko or any of the five other players with Croatian heritage in the Socceroos squad.

Viduka, who knew Šimunić from his time at Melbourne

Knights and the Australian Institute of Sport, wasn't scornful of his colleague's decision.

'Did I respect it?' he said, when I asked him about it. 'At the end of the day it was his decision. I would have loved for him to play for Australia. I remember, Joe rang me up and asked me, "What do you think I should do?" I told him he should play for Australia but he should do what he has to do. He's played in a World Cup already and the European championship, so in a career point of view he's done well.'

Put simply, as far as his friend was concerned, Šimunić had made his choice. There was nothing else to discuss.

Viduka made a different choice. It had been just as simple. He chose Australia but didn't turn his back entirely on the country of his father, Joe, who'd arrived in Melbourne as a teenager and found work butchering at Smorgon's. When Viduka captained the Young Socceroos at the world championships in Qatar in 1996, he wore an armband in Croatia's colours: red, blue and white. A gesture that could have come across as maudlin was instead poignant, almost perfect.

'I love Australia and I love playing with the boys for my country,' he said. 'When I was a young boy, my only goal was to play for Australia, and that was that. There was nothing else.'

Now in Stuttgart, where his uncle worked at the local Mercedes factory, Viduka's passion for leading his country remained undimmed. When Hiddink had approached him to be the new Socceroos captain in Honiara in late 2005, he'd felt 'chuffed and surprised, a mix of emotions'.

'I didn't have a clue that I was going to be captain before then. Guus said, "Mate, I've decided to make you captain." And I just said, "*Whoa,* thanks."'

Now Šimunić and Viduka, two men who'd made very different choices a decade ago, were walking onto opposite ends of the Gottlieb-Daimler Stadion, about to mark each other for 90 minutes for a place in the final 16 of the World Cup.

You couldn't have made it up.

Croatia was the hottest destination in travel, a place where the beautiful young people of Europe went on their summer holidays and where some of the richer ones bought holiday villas on the Istrian or Dalmatian coasts. I had toyed with the idea of taking a short break there after the football was over. The promises were suitably alluring: 'The Mediterranean As It Once Was' is the official slogan in the country's tourism ads.

Somehow, though, the placid idyll evoked by the filtered photos of deserted beaches and Roman ruins in the countryside didn't quite compute with the image its football team and their fans projected. The team's very nickname, *Vatreni,* 'The Fiery Ones', suggested an altogether different scene, one that more closely resembled recent events in the fledgling state's turbulent past.

Croatia wanted to be seen as a modern, secular, Westernised state. It was democratic, capitalist and had handed over accused war criminal (or heroic patriot, depending who you spoke to) Ante Gotovina to the International Criminal Court. It had even followed Germany's path by making it a criminal offence to praise 'fascist, Nazi and other totalitarian states and ideologies or promot[e] racism and xenophobia', specifically displaying symbols relating to the Ustaše, the murderous regime that existed under Nazi patronage during World War II.

Notably, the day of the match, 22 June, was Anti-Fascist Resistance Day, an official public holiday in Croatia. Yet the unsettling reality was that politics and nationalism were the lifeforces that fuelled Croat football.

Croatia fans had a reputation for wanton destruction—more than 100 had been arrested at Ta'Qali Stadium in Malta during qualifying, and thugs ran amok in Mostar, Bosnia-Herzegovina, after the *Vatreni*'s defeat in Berlin. In Stuttgart the organised fan groups were out in force—the BBB, Torcida, Kohorta, Demoni, Tornado—but they weren't causing trouble. Perhaps, like everyone else in Germany, the bad apples simply couldn't get tickets.

There are some great national anthems that never fail to stir—the Welsh 'Mae Hen Wlad Fy Nhadau' ('The Land of My Fathers') and the French 'La Marseillaise'—but 'Lijepa Naša Domovino' ('Our Beautiful Homeland') must surely top the list. Baroque and turgid, it's the kind of thing you'd expect to hear before going into battle against an army of the dead. The opening lines verge on militaristic, and it's a wonder they weren't banned like everything else at the World Cup:

Oj junačka zemljo mila,
Stare slave djedovino,
Da bi vazda sretna bila!

(Our beautiful homeland,
Oh dear, heroic land,
Fatherland of ancient glory,
May you always be happy!)

'We've golden soil and wealth for toil/Our home is girt by sea' was hardly a shattering riposte to a quasi-war cry, but the Aussie fans weren't deterred. As the many customised supporters' flags in the stands—Eureka, Casula Boys, Canberra Arrows, Pagewood FC—fluttered in the cool summer night, they positively belted out 'Advance Australia Fair'. Whoever had called ours a lame-duck anthem obviously hadn't heard it sung at a World Cup.

Perhaps nerves got the better of him, for with almost his first touch Viduka mistimed a midfield pass to Vince Grella, who failed to trap the ball and was burgled by Niko Kovac. The Socceroos captain, eager to make up for his mistake, ran after the veteran midfielder and crudely brought him down five metres from the 18-yard box, gifting Darijo Srna a direct free kick. Seconds later, the Shakhtar Donetsk midfielder had smacked the right corner of Kalac's net so hard the ball cannoned back onto the pitch as if this were a game of squash, not football.

There was nothing the goalkeeper could have done; indeed, it was one of those rare strikes that compel you to just sit and take a couple of slow, deep breaths before applauding its perfection. Then instinct returns. Sheer naked hatred takes over. Your team is a goal down and the clock says 02:10. How do the Socceroos dig themselves out of this mess, just when you'd started believing that maybe this wasn't all some elaborate joke, Australia being here? You have no idea, nor do those 11 guys on the pitch, but you know what you have to do now—you're not going to stop screaming till it's all over.

Immediately the Australians took to the long ball to counter the Croatian superiority in midfield, which saw the *Vatreni* fall back in defence and brought the muscular and effective Viduka into the game. Clueless about how to match his speed and guile, the Croatian defenders resorted to treachery. Stjepan Tomas knocked down the Socceroos captain with his left hand, while Šimunić, his slicked-back hair and three-day growth making him look like one of Christopher Moltisanti's deadbeat mates from *The Sopranos,* brazenly used *both* hands to tackle his old friend as if he were a dummy half tearing away from the base of a rugby league scrum. It was one of the most craven acts of foul play ever seen in a game of football, perhaps even worse than the two-handed job similarly inflicted on Viduka in the Iran game in Melbourne in 1997, but English referee Graham Poll refused to award the Australian anything but a shake of the head. When I asked Viduka about it after the game, he stuck to diplomatic niceties: 'Everybody's competitive. I don't hold it against anyone.'

Mile Sterjovski and Brett Emerton, backing up from Brazil, were harder to catch. Sterjovski, the Basel winger and favourite of Frank Farina, had expected to miss a place in the Australia squad for the World Cup but had been startlingly recalled by Hiddink. Now he was ripping shreds off the Croatians. He executed a brilliant one-touch volley from a Culina long pass to centre for Viduka in the box, only for the big guy to be brought down by Šimunić. Later in the half, down the same flank, he collected a 40-metre downfield lob from Grella, backheeled to himself, turned Marko Babić inside out, and then crossed a low bouncing shot into the box to Viduka's feet.

Emerton's key moment came when he chipped from inside the Australian half to Tim Cahill, who made a short pass to Culina on the wing. Culina then tickled it back on to Emerton, who pushed it with his left foot to Craig Moore, freeing up Emerton to canter forward. Moore passed to Kewell, and Kewell laid it up for Emerton, who took it sweetly with one touch and threaded a perfect ball through to Viduka. An Emerton cross from the same wing drew Australia's first goal. Dario Šimić handled Cahill in the box and Tomas made a blatant handball trying to head it away. The penalty for Moore was easy pickings.

It had been an extraordinary recovery by the Socceroos, appropriate reward for 30-plus minutes of sustained, relentless pressure. As in the Brazil game, the only serious flaw in their play was an almost complete lack of penetration from corners. Scott Chipperfield had taken over the duties from Culina, but the results were depressingly familiar. Without a good corner taker, it was like the Australians wanted to make winning just about as difficult as possible. But these were guys who were used to doing things the hard way.

In the second half the Australians moved up another gear, upfield forays by Neill, Emerton and Kewell creating the illusion that the game was as good as over.

It was hard to believe Brazil had been dominated by Croatia in Berlin. But one good shot in open play had reversed that equation, and one good shot in open play was what the Australians were missing. Without it, every glorious, exhilarating stride down the park counted for nothing.

Especially when they went another goal down. Kalac made an awful spill for the Croatians' second, but in fairness there were two other factors that allowed the situation to pass: Cahill's poor marking of Kovač and the fact that the Croatian's strike went through Moore's legs. The AC Milan goalkeeper didn't get a decent look before the ball skidded into him.

There was no doubt Kalac was rattled, though, almost from the time he was picked ahead of Schwarzer. The controversial decision had gone in Kalac's favour because of his supposed superior aerial ability. It was the culmination of 14 years' hard slog, first as the third-stringer behind Mark Bosnich and Schwarzer, then, when Bosnich's career was immolated in an inferno of hard drugs and egomania, as back-up to Schwarzer. Now, after all the hardship and thankless travelling, all those economy flights with kneecaps almost touching his forehead, he was in goal for Australia's most important game ever. But the unstoppable bullet from Srna had shaken his confidence. He'd almost fumbled the ball over the line in the 40th minute from a simple flighted corner, also from Srna. Now, 20 minutes on, he'd committed a goalkeeper's cardinal sin—the howler.

'The ball just bounced in front of me—and I didn't get my top hand over the top of it—flicked the top of my hand and it's gone up and spun back in,' he told me later. 'One of those goals you just don't wish on anyone.'

Hiddink's dangerous bluff had come unstuck, but there was still 25 minutes left to salvage a draw. The game had entered a critical phase. Croatia seemed indolent, content to sit back and push the ball around. They'd obviously not been watching the tapes of Australia's past few games. Hiddink seized the initiative: John Aloisi came on for Grella, Mark Bresciano for Sterjovski, Josh Kennedy for Chipperfield. The momentum shifted instantly. Bresciano, from the moment he ran onto the field, took over the running of the game. Corners and free kicks assumed their rightful menace. Rising for one trademark Bresciano dipper, Tomas again handballed in the box, this indiscretion even more blatant than the one that had earned Australia's goal in the first half—it was a move from beach volleyball.

But Poll refused to award a free. A lesser team might have lost heart then and there, packed it in, but the Socceroos refused to countenance defeat, rushing the forward line. All the invention was theirs. Even when Croatia were on the counterattack and space would open up, they were able to calmly close down the opposition. Against Iran at the MCG in 1997, at the same stage of the game, such tactics had proved beyond their capability. But this was a different Australia. There was ambition, experience and skill. Hiddink's unbreakable self-confidence, his Chili Palmer-like coolness, was showing off in his team. It was just a matter of being patient.

The leveller came from a flighted Bresciano ball into the box that shaved Aloisi's head and fell behind to where Kewell, who shouldn't have even been on the park—the plan had been to keep him on for 60 minutes—was in a marginally offside position. The strike was clinical, but his reaction wasn't. It was a look we'd seen on highlight reels of his glory days at Leeds United, a look he reserved for moments when he'd pulled off some unthinkably audacious piece of magic. That look seemed so long ago. But here it was again. The open mouth. The closed eyes. The tensed jugulars. The pumping fists. The white noise. This was more than a goal. It was a purging.

The tense, hair-trigger edginess of the contest descended into violence and chaos. Igor Tudor received the ball in front of the Aussie goal from a long cross from wide out and shot straight, with Kalac marooned alone in goal, but Emerton wrapped himself around his shooting leg and Neill got a touch from his boot in a last-gasp lunge to allow Moore to clear away on the goal line. A minute later, Kovać spooned a cross straight at Kalac, who collected cleanly but threw straight at midfielder Jerko Leko, who clobbered a fairway drive into the bleachers. Substitute striker Luka Modrić had a clear shot outside the box but clipped Aloisi's right boot to push it outside the left post. The Australian fans could barely look at the field. They'd seen so many games lost when the game was as good as over.

Poll had by now lost whatever control he'd had. Šimić and Emerton had been sent off for second yellows. Šimunić rugby-tackled Viduka for a second time, then, for the hell of it, did the same to Kennedy. A second yellow meant he too was gone, but in the verbal altercation that followed, Šimunić somehow escaped being sent off. (It wasn't the first time 'The Thing from Tring' had stuffed up in the tournament; in South Korea's opening game against Togo he'd produced a red card before a second yellow when he sent off the Sparrow Hawks' Jean-Paul Abalo.) Moments later, the slippery Kennedy was again thrown to the ground, this time just metres from the goal. Aloisi collected the stray ball and put it into the net but the whistle had gone. Was the game over? Was the goal allowed? Was Australia penalised?

Kewell was just as mystified as anyone. 'I thought it was a goal. I didn't know what had happened,' he told me afterwards. 'I was celebrating, then I said, "What?", then I'd start back, then I was celebrating, then I stopped. I didn't know what was going on.'

Poll blew his whistle for the final time: 2-2. Viduka rushed to embrace him. Šimunić taunted the Englishman for not sending him off. Poll shoved him aside, stepped a few paces off to his right, rummaged in his shorts and thrust another yellow into the air—Šimunić's third. A red then materialised from his shirt pocket. It was the correct card but four minutes too late. Watching the *Vatreni* self-destruct was like watching a feral cat being hit by a car. They wobbled, snarled, clawed at the air, then they were dead. Bodies lay scattered everywhere. The army of the dead had been slayed.

As AC/DC's 'You Shook Me All Night Long' thumped from the ground speakers (a brilliant choice—whoever picked the playlist that night will live in infamy), a lone Croatian fan stood silently at the front of the media stand, holding aloft the national flag. He didn't move for 30 minutes.

CHAPTER SIX · GROSSO POINT BLANK

'The truth lies on the field.'

GREECE COACH OTTO REHHAGEL

The morning after the miracle in Stuttgart, I walked up the Rue des Grandes Arcades in Strasbourg and bought the international edition of *The Guardian* and whatever other English rags I could find. The British papers had gone batty-eyed over Mark Viduka, a surprising turnaround given they generally thought him one of the laziest, fattest and most ineffective players in the Premiership. But not even the most cynical hack on Fleet Street could deny he'd had a great game befitting a captain, and the reports were full of praise for his team. Even more optimistically, these being British papers, there was talk England could meet its recalcitrant colony in the final. They wished.

Back home, a photo of John Howard leaping from his chair after Craig Moore's equaliser added weight to the notion that the Socceroos had breached that once-impervious barrier to become part of the mainstream. Football was no longer just the stupid passion of a bunch of deluded journos and a few thousand dateless fans who should have known better. Now, with Italy lying ahead in Kaiserslautern on 26 June, it was Australia's stupid passion too.

The mood even in Italy, spiritual home of the cocky footballer, was such that anything was possible for Australia. Memories of Korea-Japan 2002, where the Italians had come unstuck at the same stage against Hiddink's Taeguk Warriors in a 2–1 golden-goal thriller, were still fresh.

That result, the highlight of the previous World Cup for many, had destroyed the career of the Ecuadorian referee, got the Korean goal scorer the sack from his Italian club, and spawned more conspiracy theories than the death of Princess Diana. Against Australia, Italy wasn't facing a Germany or a France or a Brazil—teams that could automatically strike fear into Italian hearts—but defeats to the two Koreas in 1966 and 2002 had proved no one, least of all an 'Asian' team, could be underestimated.

As sports journalist Gaia Piccardi warned in a piece for Italy's leading daily, *Corriere della Sera,* before Hiddink came along, Australian football had been '*uno sport per signorine*'—a sport for little girls. That was no more. With '*il mago*', that wizard, in charge, if Italy weren't smart the Socceroos could pull another Korea.

Australia's big day necessitated a return to Kaiserslautern, but this time around I took the train from Strasbourg. Jamo and Harro had happily returned to Australia the day after the Croatia game, feeling they couldn't ask for more than they'd already received from their two weeks in Germany. After getting daily SMS updates of the Socceroos mania engulfing Australia, they wanted a taste of what it was like on the other side—to watch the World Cup at home, to wake up in the middle of the night, wrap themselves in a beanie and scarf, and party hard with their mates at Wheeler Place in Newcastle. They'd been waiting all their lives for something like this.

I arrived early, before 8 am, and the concourse outside the station was deserted. In town, shop vendors were putting out their displays of cheap plastic flags, knockoff jerseys and other hideous trinkets. By late afternoon, though, the streets were packed with rival groups of fans drinking beer, eating sausages and bantering good-naturedly about how they were going to rip each other to pieces at five o'clock. It was a clash of civilisations in more ways than football. Many of the Aussie supporters were getting around in yellow T-shirts featuring a road sign of a drunk crawling on his knees beneath the slogan 'SOCCEROOS KAISERSLAUTERN GERMANY 2006—AUSSIES CROSSING'. Some of the Italians, meanwhile, had dressed as if they were about to go clubbing.

At the stadium, it was business as usual. When the players came out to inspect the pitch, Viduka took some time out from listening to his iPod and walked over to the crowd to kiss his son, Joey, and pose for happy snaps. Zeljko Kalac followed. For a game in which they were without their two most effective impact players—Harry Kewell courtesy of a phantom injury and Brett Emerton through suspension—the team seemed remarkably relaxed.

As had been announced the previous day, Mark Schwarzer replaced Kalac and took up his position between goal to do some warm-up drills. Mark Bresciano chatted with some of the Italian players. Downfield, the world's most expensive goalkeeper, Juventus's Gianluigi Buffon, ran onto the pitch and, arms raised, did a Rocky Balboa-like jig to a rapturous ovation.

A show of another kind was going on in the stands. Twenty metres away from the media seats, in the VIP box where Sepp Blatter and Franz Beckenbauer were vigorously pumping hands, some of the biggest powerbrokers in Australian sport were hurrying to their seats: Frank Lowy and his sons; James Packer; former federal sports minister Rod Kemp. Whatever happened over the next 90 minutes, their presence was a sign that Australian football was at last on the front foot.

Right from the kickoff, it was clear the Socceroos had a markedly different game plan. As the commentator for ESPN Gamecast's live blog joked: 'Australia have lined up with what seems to be a 3-1-4-1-1 formation—possibly.'

It was also immediately apparent that, unlike the chaos of the Japan game and the end-to-end action of Brazil and Croatia, the Socceroos seemed content to slow things down a bit. Given the disparity in the squads' quality I had thought Hiddink might revert to some of the tried and true strategies of Australian football—tight man-marking, crunching tackles—as the only way to handle the Italians, but the Australians kept a respectful distance, pushing the ball around like they were office mates having a kickaround on their lunch break.

The illusion only lasted a few minutes. On their first move upfield the *Azzurri* had the Socceroos in all sorts of trouble when Alessandro Del Piero got the ball deep down near the left corner flag and, stalling it with his left instep, caused Jason Culina, who was tracking back, to fractionally misposition himself. Del Piero stroked the ball aside with the same foot and beat his man with a cross to striker Luca Toni, who evaded Scott Chipperfield. Toni's header went outside the right post by a foot. Schwarzer would easily have been beaten if it had been on target.

With the midfield as passable as a Himalayan border post in winter, both teams began testing each other's defences with long balls. A hard, low Marco Materazzi pass upfield found Toni, who played in Del Piero. His cross to Simone Perrotta ended up behind the Roma player's legs yet still he managed to lay it off to Alberto Gilardino, whose shot crashed into Chipperfield's outstretched leg.

More aerial pingpong followed. With the Australian defence rushing forward and left short at the back, Gennaro Gattuso delivered an exquisitely flighted pass to Toni, who headed on to Gilardino. But with the onrushing Neill about to close him down, he was forced into making a side-on bicycle kick at head height.

Schwarzer tipped the shot over the crossbar with both hands, falling back like he'd been hit by a dumping wave, which was exactly what the remorseless Italians were proving to be. Minutes later, Pirlo lobbed a pass from metres inside the halfway line to Toni, who turned his back to Grella, poked the ball with his right foot, then swivelled around and smacked a low shot with his left. Only Schwarzer's right boot saved a certain goal.

Australia's chances, and half-ones at best, were few and far between. Chipperfield cantered down the left wing and somehow slipped the ball past two defenders while lying on the ground to Viduka, but the Australian captain did one backheel too many and was snaffled by Gianluca Zambrotta. Viduka also got his head onto a Mark Bresciano free kick, but hit it straight at Buffon. Another Bresciano free resulted in an unexpected opportunity when the ball slipped off Moore's backside in the box and sat up for Chipperfield who was steaming down the left unmarked. Again, though, the shot thudded right into Buffon.

The *Azzurri* had done what Australia's other opponents had failed to do: nullified its strength, its flanks. And in trying to counter the midfield lobs of Pirlo, the Australians were being forced to play deep in defence, opening up space where there should have been none.

AC Milan's playmaker was on another level entirely. According to *The New York Times*' Roger Cohen, by the end of the tournament Pirlo had touched the ball 632 times, 203 more than Zinedine Zidane. This sort of *Il Fantasista* player, a ball-controlling creative playmaker, was something Australia had lacked at the World Cup. Bresciano was talented enough to fulfil that role but had been reduced to cameos. The only other player in the squad who could have played the part was Josip Skoko, but there wasn't much he could do about it, cooling his heels on the bench.

Italian coach Marcello Lippi clearly had the edge, so Hiddink decided to change tack. The Australians went out for the second half intent not to give up possession as easily. To make the Italians work for the ball. To keep it on the deck. Every second Pirlo didn't have the ball was another second towards extra-time, something Lippi wanted to avoid. Off came Gilardino, on came Vincenzo Iaquinta, a taller, heavier striker.

Within minutes, Iaquinta had got around Neill deep on the

right wing and sent a searing low cross into the Australian box; Toni sprayed the rebound over the bar.

Lippi's second substitution was forced on him. Materazzi, the stand-in for the injured Alessandro Nesta, caught Bresciano's trailing leg in a mistimed tackle and was sent off, prompting a straight striker-defender switch. This was where Hiddink would normally have played his first trump card—Kewell. But he was on crutches. What other player was right for the job? Josh Kennedy was not really suited to the opposition; the world-class Italian defence would be adroit at shutting him out. Hiddink needed a dribbler, an attacking player to smash up the *Azzurri* fortress down the centre of the pitch. Emerton could do it, but he was suspended. The alternatives—Stan Lazaridis, Archie Thompson, Skoko—hadn't kicked a ball all tournament. Throwing them on now, with everything on the line, would be risky. John Aloisi, an out-and-out striker, was the only other option. The minutes ticked over. A decision had to be made. But Hiddink chose to just sit.

'Guus is a gambler,' said Graham Arnold. 'He plays this Dutch game called *toepen,* where you risk everything on the last card. You only get four cards. It basically summed up how he coaches. It was a massive gamble to leave Harry out in Sydney. It was a massive gamble to play Kalac ahead of Schwarzer. He gambled against Italy—and still to this day I've never actually sat down and spoken to him after the game about things—but I said to him with 15 to 20 minutes to go: "Do you think it's time to get Josh on?"

'And he said: "We get them in extra-time." He gambled to keep the two fresh subs up our sleeve for extra-time to apply the gas at the end, 'cause he said physically we'll run over the top of them.'

Whether he was being cautious or playing a high-risk game—most likely somewhere between the two—Hiddink's strategy appeared prescient, with Neill rushing down the left, taking a pass from Bresciano and sending a square pass to Chipperfield unmarked on the edge of the box. He spun around and shot hard and straight but Buffon positioned himself perfectly. Now, with Italy a man down, the Australian flanks had been liberated. Everything was happening down the wings.

With 20 minutes to go, Australia had all the momentum. Italy was sitting back, happy to absorb the pressure and then spring forward on the counterattack. But when Francesco Totti came on for Del Piero five minutes later, it was a signal that Lippi hadn't given up. Totti had been an underperformer for his team and was still playing himself back into form after breaking the fibula in his left leg and sustaining ankle ligament tears in a Serie A match four months before. His rehabilitation had been a national soap opera, Italy's unpopular prime minister Silvio Berlusconi, who also happened to be AC Milan's president, deigning to visit the injured Roma captain by his bedside. It wasn't enough to keep him in office.

Yet with almost his first touch outside the 18-yard box Totti had four Aussies around him and still managed to cross inside with his left foot to Perrotta. Only Neill's quick thinking and hard buttocks stopped an unlikely winner. The pressure switched back to the Aussies. Bresciano had one half-chance but duffed his strike, Viduka was doing his tricks but had no one around him to capitalise on the space he was creating, and Cahill got a clean header but donked it over the bar.

Finally, with just nine minutes left in normal time, Hiddink made his move. Mile Sterjovski was off, Aloisi on. How many times had Aloisi been in this position? You could look at his 40-odd appearances in the green and gold since 1997, and his 20-odd goals, and deduce he was a reasonable striker. But if you consider he'd played the lion's share of those games as a replacement, often getting little more than 15 minutes to make an impact, his stats start looking even better.

'In the [1997 and 2001] World Cup campaigns I played a total of five minutes in the four games. That was upsetting,' he told me. 'But you know that whenever you get the chance you have to perform, so you have to have confidence in your own ability.

'That's where you have to be mentally strong. Sometimes I think I should be playing and I'm not, but every player thinks they should always be playing. When I get that chance I like to *show* that I should be playing.'

Aloisi's assignment here, though, called not just for a goal but for delicacy. It was to bag the winner while not turning over possession. For every attempt on Buffon's goal, the Aussies would have to defend on the counter. Italy was renowned for pulling out results when the chips were stacked against them.

'I think the send-off of Materazzi may have cost us,' said Craig Foster. 'You knew Italy would close up. If anyone's going to put ten men behind the ball in the world, the best at it—and the one you don't want to have to play against to try to break down—is Italy.'

Rale Rasic, Australia's 1974 World Cup coach, agreed: 'Marcello Lippi was reduced to ten men and he knew how to sell half of the field. Straightaway he put it on the market for sale. Dropped two strikers. Played with ten men in his own half, introduced Totti when he was needed, and attacked only with Grosso and Zambrotta. You analyse Lippi's tournament, this was the first time in the history of football that one coach attacked with a left fullback and a right fullback.'

Hang on, who was playing total football here? Bresciano slammed a left-footed strike around Italy's left-back Fabio Grosso but the ball sailed way over Buffon. A couple of times the Italians looked close to scoring on the counter, but frantic manning of Schwarzer's goalmouth prevented an upset goal. The best chance came when Aloisi, true to his flash-in-the-pan reputation, sheared his legs into the air and pulled off a spectacular bicycle kick attempt in the 89th minute, but missed the ball completely. It quickly returned to the Italians' possession. There was just 30 seconds to go.

What happened next, not Grosso's infamous penalty, was where Australia made its big mistake. While Viduka and

Gattuso were jostling on the Italian side of the halfway line over some piffling disagreement, Totti, marked by Cahill, was left on the ball for a total of *eight* seconds. It might not sound like much, but at that stage of the game, with a sudden-death World Cup match on the line, it's a major error. Worse, it was one Hiddink had repeatedly warned the Australians to be vigilant about. While fatigued during training sessions, some of the Aussies had reverted to their old habits of not tracking and closing down players. Now they were doing it in the biggest game of their lives.

'For Totti, Maradona, Pelé, Ronaldinho, eight seconds is equivalent to eight minutes,' said Rasic. 'Players like Totti need just a split-second to solve all the problems of the world. That's why they are special.'

In that short amount of time, Totti could see there were three Australian players in or just outside the centre circle marking three Italian players. Ahead of them were three Australians marking three Italians, with one Australian high up the park marking nobody. At the last line of defence, there were two Australians marking two men, Grosso on the left and Iaquinta in the centre, yet one more Australian player on the right flank was on his own. Totti correctly judged the percentages lay with getting a pass down to Grosso on the left, where he had only one man to beat, Bresciano, the wrong man in the wrong position. If Grosso could get around him, he would only have Neill and Iaquinta in front of him, and Schwarzer in goal.

Totti was cultured enough to deliver the perfect pass, and he did, the ball bouncing just ahead of where Grosso was trying to lose Bresciano. Grosso took two touches and with his third made a feint to suggest he was going to the line but cut the ball back in, leaving Bresciano off balance and making him go to ground. Neill, who'd moved away from Iaquinta to deny Grosso a direct shot at goal, with Moore covering for him, blocked the defender's run but overextended his leg by half a yard, simple gravity dictating he had to fall to the grass.

God forbid the decision be analysed again—football fans have yet to decide whether Geoff Hurst's second goal in the 1966 World Cup final was legitimate—but even if a case were made for obstruction, Spanish referee Luis Medina Cantalejo was heavy-handed in awarding a direct free kick when an indirect kick would have been the proper sanction. In going to ground, Neill technically 'impeded the progress of an opponent', but in any fair assessment of the situation Grosso threw himself on Neill's prostrate body, meaning the Australian could not really be at fault for the nature of the ensuing contact.

The fact remains, however, that Neill was there to be tripped over, so ultimately Neill must accept responsibility for what happened, which to this day he selflessly does. Such is football. It was a tragedy for the Socceroos, and a personal tragedy for Neill, but the greatest tragedy of all was still to come. That was when Australia, like Italy, England and Portugal before it, developed its own World Cup persecution myth.

When FIFA president Sepp Blatter later apologised for the Grosso penalty on Australian television, and even said the Socceroos should have gone to the quarters in place of the Italians, it became official. The fact that Blatter quickly retracted his comments when the Italian press got in a flap about it only gave the conspiracy theory more currency.

A persecution myth is the last thing the Socceroos wanted in their baggage when they left Germany. With one, though, nobody could ever accuse us of not being a football nation.

An hour later, in the mixed zone, Arnold was already at it, muttering about how Australia was 'a small footballing nation that gets no favours' and 'all we asked for was a fair go, and I don't think we received it over the four games'. Tim Cahill was pushing the same line: 'I just can't believe it, mate. I'm furious. The luck we've had with referees at this World Cup, everything's been against us and we've fought hard to make everything work for us and in the end it doesn't work for us. All that hard work

... one decision has changed everything. It's changed Australian football. It's changed our lives.' Viduka complained about a handball from Zambrotta in the final minutes that wasn't given: 'Somehow we don't get these decisions.'

Others were more philosophical. Vince Grella thought the Socceroos were 'stronger' than Italy, 'at about the 70-minute mark they were starting to die down', but the *Azzurri* 'tactically were very intelligent because they sort of always were leaving us with a wing free but we weren't really taking advantage of it. They were boxing up the area, but even [when we were] a man up they could break us down.' Said Aloisi: 'They weren't better than us. They got through because they had more experience. They were probably more street smart ... you don't want to go out of the World Cup like that but it's gone and we just have to try and get over it.' Schwarzer was more blunt: 'We had one hell of a chance to go through and we didn't take it.'

The players were holding up better than some of the journalists. Anita Bulan, producer of *The Away Game* documentary, was beside herself. Comedy writer Santo Cilauro was in tears. 'That's why it's beautiful—it's so cruel,' he said morosely. I wasn't sure whether he was joking. Others were trying to be brave, saying that this was a result we needed to have. That injustice was all part of the game. Australia's beautiful innocence had got us this far; only hard-hearted guile could take us further.

I asked Cahill what impact he thought Australia had had on the tournament.

'Everything. Honesty. Discipline. Bright. Colourful,' he said. 'We like having a laugh. We've been ourselves. We shouldn't be overawed by these games. We've earned enough respect to play what we've played and we've done really well, so it just goes to show how far Australia has come as a nation. Maybe we're too honest. Maybe so, maybe not. The thing is, we'd prefer to go out of a World Cup with our heads held up high than to just stay in it. We've rocked the nation. We've rocked the world. It's all good.'

Aloisi, though, wasn't thinking much beyond how he was going to get through the night. 'The world's taken notice that we're no mugs. We got through a tough group. We earned a lot of respect.' He paused a beat. 'But at the moment it doesn't mean too much.'

The 2006 World Cup is already being remembered as the tournament where defence triumphed over attack, where creativity was stifled by *catenaccio.* Lippi's *Azzurri* would win the final against France in Berlin on 9 July unconvincingly, Zinedine Zidane's brain snap gifting them a victory they scarcely deserved. The best teams, after all, don't always win World Cups.

For me, though, the tournament was all about heroic failure, and no teams represented this more than the Socceroos and their hosts, Germany. The result in Kaiserslautern on 26 June was greeted with unexpected shock and anger around the world, and for once an Australian sporting team was looked upon with some sympathy. Though the ending of the story was not kind to Australia, we left Germany as one of the few 'fairytales' of a competition that didn't spring the hoped-for surprises of World Cups past. Even *La Gazzetta dello Sport,* Italy's notoriously partisan sports rag, had the grace to admit Grosso's penalty was 'doubtful' and Italy's progression in the tournament seemed 'marked by Providence'.

More heartening news was to follow. Information Builders, a British software company, released an alternative set of data to FIFA's Fair Play Index called the 'IBI Foul Play Index', which collated dives, intimidation of referees, fake injuries, even players failing to sing national anthems during the four weeks of football. Italy topped the dive count on 40, with Portugal second on 30. Australia came in with eight dives. They placed equal 22nd.

As for Jürgen Klinsmann's team, they produced the best attacking football of the tournament, overturning all the cliches about the dourness of the country's football and repositioning Germany's brand, as their coach promised he would. It was extraordinary to think there'd been calls for Klinsmann to appear before parliamentary committees prior to the World Cup to explain how he was going to win it. He didn't appear, nor did he win it, the *Nationalmannschaft* finishing third after bowing out to Italy in a pulsating match in Dortmund—Grosso again playing the spoiler. Such was the feeling of elation about the spirit in which his team played, though, that in the days following the game Klinsmann could have run for chancellor and won hands down.

Before leaving Australia for the World Cup, I'd attended a grim German National Tourist Board promotion at Sydney's Hilton Hotel. The audience, which included a smattering of bored sports journalists, were told Germany wanted to be seen as 'modern', 'open to the world', 'a place for business opportunities' and a 'world champion in experts'. Above all, they assured us unconvincingly, 'We want to be LOVABLE!'

I was sceptical the host country could achieve *any*—certainly not all—of their aims in just four weeks, but when it was all over the World Cup had lifted the veil of darkness that post-war democracy, consumerism and enforced pacifism could not. The German people couldn't recover what they had lost because of the Nazis, but these four weeks of football showed they could celebrate what they still had.

That said, the security could have eased up a bit. For all their desire to make friends, the World Cup organisers still showed an over-zealous and sometimes absurd adherence to the rules—Dutch fans in orange *lederhosen* were stripped to their underwear in Cologne, all because the logo on the front was from a brewery that wasn't an 'official partner'. Still, they fared better than Bruno, the only brown bear to pass into German territory for nearly 200 years. His shooting was the biggest story outside the World Cup. When asked why the bear had been shot, Otmar Bernhard, Bavaria's deputy environment minister, told reporters: 'It's not that we don't welcome bears in Bavaria. It's just that this one wasn't behaving properly.'

Germany's great rival, France, began poorly but by the second round were playing the sort of football Brazil promised but didn't deliver. The resurrection of the legend of Zidane became the main narrative for the world's media in the lead-up to the final, but it was the team itself that was the great story. After hobbling into the second round, the superannuated *Les Bleus* proceeded to embarrass the Spaniards, Brazilians and Portuguese with their exquisite skill and superb control in midfield, though Thierry Henry disgraced himself with dives against Spain (a feigned blow from Carlos Puyol) and Portugal (an innocuous ankle tap from Ricardo Carvalho that prompted him to throw himself into the air as if jumping off a bridge). The player Henry had lambasted in France's opening game, Franck Ribery, emerged as one of the stars of the tournament.

As is often the case at the World Cup, the so-called 'lesser' ties, such as Saudi Arabia vs Tunisia, Angola vs Mexico or South Korea vs Togo, captivated. Perhaps it was because these teams had everything to play for and nothing to lose. (That, or I was simply watching too much football.) The players seemed more agile, more prepared to take risks. Everything that football's first-world nations—especially tortured, timid England—so conspicuously lacked. As Roger Cohen cracked: '[Sven-Goran] Eriksson's gone now into the Scandinavian night. He deserves to shiver there for a while.' Some of the 'bigger' ties, of course, did come very close to delivering real drama, such as Ivory Coast vs Argentina and Brazil vs Croatia, but the much-hyped blockbuster in the historic grudge-match stakes, Germany vs Poland, proved to be an unmitigated bore.

Of the Socceroos' opponents in Group F, Japan would ultimately return to Narita with just one point from three games. Yet it all could have turned out so differently—leading Australia for over 80 minutes, blowing a gilt-edged chance in their nil-all draw with the cocky Croatians, going a goal up against a scoreless Brazil from debutant Keiji Tamada's superb long-range strike.

Rather than accept responsibility for his tactical mistakes, Zico sheeted blame to tournament organisers for unfavourable kickoff times and to his players for their height, and intimated it had all been impossible anyway. Asian football, he wagered, was never going to be any good until the Asian leagues were on a par with Europe (conveniently not mentioning Hiddink's achievements in 2002). Within a week he was the new coach of Turkish club Fenerbahce, making the same sort of promises he failed to keep with Japan. Football's coaching merry-go-round went on.

Brazil would walk away bruised and humiliated in its tussle with *oba oba*. In 2005, I'd choked on a pork knuckle as I watched Brazil's attack—Ronaldinho, Adriano, Kaká, Robinho—murder Argentina in the Confederations Cup final, four goals to one.

They had made the *Albicelestes*, the world's second-best team, look like an under-11 boys' park side from Launceston. It was at once the most thrilling and most disturbing game of football I'd ever seen. They were a *galaxy* apart in class. Unfortunately for the World Cup organisers, that same team didn't play in 2006. This one had Ronaldo, who had given himself a holiday while his team-mates tore apart German pitches the year before.

Despite a tsunami of Nike ambush marketing, the world wasn't fooled by Brazil. The greatest fools were the Brazilian players themselves, who had started to believe that just turning up to their games guaranteed a clear passage to the final in Berlin. Their insouciance was perfectly summed up when Roberto Carlos adjusted his socks in the quarter-final defeat to France just as Zidane was lining up his free kick. Zidane spotted the bent Carlos and connected with Henry, who volleyed the ball into the net unimpeded. And with that bizarre goal, the world champions were out of the tournament. Despite this, Carlos Alberto Parreira, who had the gall to declare that his team 'dealt well with the favouritism', walked into a four-year deal with South Africa on a cool US$250,000 a month. Nice work if you can get it.

In Munich, the Brazilian media was still in awe of their team, despite obvious signs that all was not well. Carlos and Ronaldo slinked through the mixed zone like movie stars pausing to sign autographs at a premiere. But in Stuttgart, refreshingly, the Croatian media wouldn't have a bar of any attitude from their players. Following their capitulation to the Socceroos, Dado Pršo and Niko Kranjčar shot straight through the mixed zone, heads down, not prepared to say anything to anyone. But they were taken to task—loudly. Fists were shaken, insults thrown. It looked like it would come to blows. Croatian football writers could be even fierier than their football team.

Croatia's coach, Zlatko Kranjčar, who refused to admit he'd erred, saying his team was undone by bad luck, was sacked within two weeks of his return to Croatia and replaced by former World Cup defender and national under-21s coach Slaven Bilić.

A rattled Graham Poll took a short break from refereeing but returned to the park in early August for Colchester United's loss to Barnsley. The fans had suitable fun at his expense. 'Two more! He only needs two more!' one wag cried when Colchester midfielder Kemal Izzet was given a yellow. Poll is now officiating again in the English Premier League.

Putting the eventual world champions to the sword wasn't enough to keep some of the Socceroos from ruling out retirement. Viduka was bitterly disappointed at the manner of Australia's elimination, and had refused even before the World Cup to be drawn on whether he would commit to further games with the national team. From his hangdog look in Kaiserslautern, though, it appeared he'd all but had his mind made up for him.

'For myself it will be very demanding, on everybody as players,' he said. 'I'm curious to see if I've got the drive and determination [to get to 2010]. My number-one priority is my family.'

As shattered players returned to their clubs for pre-season training or took a few precious days off for holidays with their partners and families, none of the European-based professionals who got game time in Germany officially declared their international careers were over. Some, including Schwarzer, didn't hesitate to state their intention to back up for another World Cup campaign.

My own feelings were of relief. Getting so far in a World Cup requires nerves, stamina and a preparedness to have your heart broken. As any football fan knows, whatever your team, whatever the competition, there comes a point where you're going to get hurt—*badly*. In a World Cup, that pain is compounded many times over.

The Socceroos proved that losing can sometimes be positive. The fact that Italian players and team management could look at the slow-mo replay of Grosso falling down so theatrically over Neill and feel not the slightest bit of shame going into the next round said something about the culture of Italian football. Conversely, the way Neill dealt with his anguish, and the way his team-mates rallied around him, said something about our own. Had he been playing centre-back for England or Portugal, Neill would most probably have been crucified for his mistake.

As Rasic told me later when we discussed the incident: 'Sport is something that requires pride and honour. Winning is not everything. *Honour in winning* is greater than winning itself. Historically Aussies are not the best losers, but we know how to handle failure, and we proved to the world that we can be great in defeat.'

This, the way we accepted our elimination, not our unexpected progression, was how Australia found acceptance as a football nation at the World Cup. The Socceroos set themselves apart with their positivity, their fearlessness and, above all, their ingrained sense of fair play in a tournament that would be marred by cheating, violence and gamesmanship. (Only once, during the course of Australia's four games, could I recall anything approaching dishonesty: when Cahill went down after an ankle tackle from Brazilian captain Cafu and clutched at his face as if he'd been splashed with acid.) Old myths were also destroyed. No longer could Australians be called 'dirty', a rabble of hackers and knuckle-dragging convicts who tore holes in opponents' shins. The Socceroos played good technical football as well as anyone and showed they could adapt to whatever system Hiddink threw at them.

Australia showed the world it was possible to play the game without cynicism or underhandedness and still win. The Socceroos may have ultimately had their football naivete exposed by a more cutthroat team, yet the players, and their supporters, wouldn't have had it any other way. This might have been the 'world game', but we still played it with Australian values first, European style second.

Frank Lowy's bold punt in appointing Hiddink a year before had paid off, just another extraordinary investment in a business career without parallel in Australia. Yet after the defeat in Kaiserslautern, Hiddink struck a dejected figure. For a footballing mercenary who had pocketed almost $4 million for his trouble, he was showing uncharacteristic attachment to his men.

'You don't realise how much I loved doing this job,' Australia's now former coach told Graham Arnold. 'A lot of jobs I do because it's a job. But I would have done this one for nothing, I enjoyed it that much.'

So did we, Guus Geluk. So did we.

After the Australian and Italian players and their entourages had finished piling onto their buses in Kaiserslautern, I realised I had lost track of time and was about to miss the last train to Strasbourg. I ran down the stairs and into the car park, where I jumped on one of the media shuttles. It was the wrong bus—in my haste I hadn't asked the driver where it was going—and ended up in another car park 20 kilometres out of the city. Fortunately, though, I wasn't the only one to have made the mistake. There were two other journos onboard. One was Richard Williams, the senior football columnist for *The Guardian*. While we were talking about the match, he took a call on his mobile. His sub-editor in London was ringing to check his copy.

'Yes, *cannoniere*—C-A-N-N-O-N-I-E-R-E,' he said, referring to the Italian word for striker. 'And you don't think it's terribly gauche of me to give man-of-the-match to Totti, do you? Well, he did make the difference.'

I could only shake my head. But that's the way truth is in football. It may lie on the field, but what two people see on a football pitch can never be the same.

When I finally reached the station, I'd missed every connecting train to the border and was told I'd have to get off in Offenburg and catch a taxi to Strasbourg. It was well past 9 pm, yet the trains were still overflowing with fans on their way back to hostels, campsites and hotel rooms. I found a space in the vestibule and sat down on the floor. Two young Japanese women were standing by the exit, both uncommonly attractive and wearing wristbands in the colours of the Italian flag. In Japan, unlike most other parts of Asia, Italy's Serie A remains the most popular European football league. As passengers filed past from carriage to carriage, a Mexican guy stopped, pointed at their wrists and gave a thumbs-up, as if to say, 'Good game'. The girls smiled politely and brushed him off, turning to look at the night lights out the window. Chastened, the Mexican guy returned to his seat.

I couldn't help but smile. It would take time—maybe decades—but one day, in another railway car late at night somewhere in Europe, those wristbands would be green and gold.

SECOND HALF · ASIAN CUP

CHAPTER SEVEN · INTO ASIA

'We have been pathetic when it comes to Asia. We are like the bloke who expects to score with a sheila he's just met: there is no courting, no relationship building, no cups of tea in the morning. We have been very guilty of the old "How about a fuck?" line. It is just not good enough.'

JOHNNY WARREN
IN *MR AND MRS SOCCER* BY ANDY HARPER (2004)

If I'd had trouble figuring out what I was supposed to do after the Socceroos qualified for the World Cup, I was clueless now that they'd been knocked out. Three decades of anguish, misery and the sort of patience that would outlast Job had been atomised into two weeks of exhilaration, joy and achievement that should have sated any football fan for three decades more. I should have been content. But it wasn't enough. I didn't want to go back to the way things were before. Like anyone who loved our national team, anyone who had been in Germany and seen the games up close, I wanted to see more of it. This had been good. This was what it was all about. We'd been right all along. The time for football in Australia had come.

If there's one thing Socceroos supporters are more used to than losing, it's waiting. After Frank Farina's side had been smashed to bits in Uruguay in November 2001, it wasn't until February 2003 that anything resembling our full-strength team played again, this time against England in that memorable 3-1 upset at Upton Park. And it wasn't until Turkey toured in May

2004 that the Socceroos came home, and that was only because the Turks, World Cup semi-finalists in 2002, had failed to qualify for the European championship. Waiting a year, two years, even longer, to see the Socceroos play, home or away, has largely been the grim lot in life of Australia's disparate football tribes, a vast expanse of time filled in with countless hours of debating team line-ups in internet chatrooms or writing hate mail to Peter FitzSimons.

I needn't have panicked. For the first time in living memory, there was more in store for fans than another four-year wait for the next World Cup. With their adventure in Germany consigned to history, the Socceroos' immediate priority was qualifying for the 2007 AFC Asian Cup. With a new home in Asia, Australian football was no longer suspended in aspic. We had other appointments to keep.

'It means more competitive games more often,' said Lucas Neill, when I asked him about the benefits of being part of the new confederation. 'Every game we're going to have to be at our best. It's going to improve everyone's standard of performance and make us get better and better because we'll always be playing tough and competitive games. Not so much tough as in coming up against hard and skilful players, but tough conditions and tough environments to play in like Iran, Bahrain, or playing on dodgy pitches. It's a good challenge. You don't get the food you want to prepare. You don't get everything your own way and then you go out and nothing goes right and everything's against you and there's 70,000 men in a stadium all in their gowns and scarves on their heads. It's crazy. It's different. It should be intimidating.'

Mark Bresciano, however, was more circumspect: 'Mate, the only bad thing is the travelling we're gonna be doing. Playing in these Asian Cups and travelling to either Asia or Australia during the international window is going to be a bit hard for us, but for me as a player and us as a team it's going to be better because we're actually going to have decent competition leading up to major tournaments. If it wasn't too safe, though, I wouldn't be going.'

I didn't care if I had to paddle through the Straits of Malacca on a palm frond—I just wanted to see the Socceroos play again. This was no longer just about football. This was about Australia closing one door and opening another. We had made a big impression in Germany, but this was going to be a more profound engagement: we were finally getting to know our own neighbourhood.

When Paul Keating made his 'banana republic' comment in 1986 he was calling for Australia to face up to the economic challenge posed by Asia. He spoke of the need for 'engagement', for cross-cultural understanding, and for Australia joining ASEAN. He had a vision for Australia *in* Asia. By 1996, though, the man with the passion for antique clocks was gone from The Lodge and Australia had halted its slow crawl north altogether.

Ten years on, the spirit of Keating's work has found an unlikely home in Australian football, the Socceroos achieving what successive foreign ministers, Labor or Liberal, have not: membership of a multilateral Asian organisation. When Australia joined the Asian Football Confederation, Frank Lowy held a press conference and announced boldly: 'This new sporting relationship with Asia will add an often missing popular dimension to Australia's relations with [its] neighbours and create new opportunities.'

A largely untrammelled frontier for Australian sport, save the rare adventures of our cricketers on the subcontinent, Asian competition would propel the Socceroos to centre stage in the fastest growing football market in the world, a continent of 3.7 billion people. The benefits weren't just limited to an easier route to the World Cup and regular international matches, but the chance to open up commercial opportunities and create business partnerships where traditional means—trade, diplomacy—had failed.

However, getting 'into Asia' as a fully paid-up member of the AFC wasn't a lightbulb that suddenly went off above Lowy's head one night in the FFA boardroom. It had been an ambition for Australian football for decades, going back to the early days of Sir Arthur George's ironfisted reign as head of the Australian Soccer Federation. In fact, it would be safe to say George desperately wanted to be part of Asia—only at the time it was a mission as futile as it was expedient. Now 92, George's recall of names is getting shaky, but his slight at the hands of the AFC in the early 1970s is something he'll never forget. As George says, 'with a little bit of help we could have become as we have become now under Lowy'. That help, however, was not forthcoming, and wasn't about to be offered anytime soon.

'I'd been invited by the former prime minister of Malaysia, Tunku Abdul Rahman, who was the AFC president, to go along to the AFC Congress before the 1974 Asian Games in Tehran and to be their guest—although I didn't turn out to be anything like a guest,' he laughed. 'When I arrived I got a smell of what was going to happen when I found my hotel reservation didn't exist anymore. I was taken some place where you almost vomited when you put your head in it.

'At the Congress, some of the members were fearful that Australia would denigrate them and make sure that no Asian won the competition. I assured them we were amateurs and were going to remain amateurs and said I'd be prepared to recommend that Australia become an associate member playing in Asia but not having a vote.

'But the next morning I got up before the Congress and before I could say two paragraphs this fellow from Kuwait made the most vicious speech about "the murderers of Taiwan, the criminals of Israel"—at that time I was pursuing a policy that anyone could play us in football—and now, according to him, Asia was about to admit the "super criminals of Australia". So the vote against us joining was carried unanimously.'

It was not taken again for another 30 years.

'We were nobodies in Asia,' George admitted ruefully. His failure still cuts deep. 'In 1973, when the Socceroos played Korea in Seoul, I was sitting in the stands and I went to go and see somebody and when I came back to my seat someone had bloody pinched it. I had to sit on the steps. That was the kind of regard they had for Australia.'

George remained as ASF president until 1988, marking nearly two decades in the job. His immediate successors, Ian Brusasco and John Constantine, would use their positions to again try wooing Asia, but met the same resistance, if not more. Especially as their overtures came at a time when there were fears that, with Australia in Asia, it would mean one less guaranteed spot in the World Cup for the continent's traditional powers.

The hostility of Malaysia and Indonesia towards Australia, which reached its zenith in the Mahathir-Keating years, was also not about to go away. One former football official who didn't want to be named said there was a longstanding attitude within the highest levels of the AFC that Australians were uncultured, insensitive, racist thugs and that this had effectively kyboshed our overtures to Asia before they'd had a chance to be heard. Brusasco described it as 'racism in reverse', saying 'there were powerful forces that didn't want us to join'.

'There was no point talking chairman to chairman, or chairman to president because it was either the shah or some other person that never really got a picture of Australia's position,' added Constantine. '[The AFC] was open to conversation but basically it went along the lines of how difficult it would be to get Charlie Dempsey's Oceania to agree when they were endeavouring to build the OFC up as a confederation.'

Brusasco's and Constantine's successor, former ABC chairman David Hill, had likewise heard the tales of George's ambush in Tehran but thought it was the responsibility of FIFA, not the AFC, to offer a balm to Australia's itch. This meant winding up the farce that was Oceania and getting the Socceroos into regular meaningful tournaments. So in 1996, looking to make a political splash, Hill voted against the ratification of the OFC as a confederation at the FIFA Congress in Zurich. Australia was roundly defeated 172 votes to one.

'We had been promised the support of Europe,' said Hill. '[Then-deputy chairman] Basil Scarsella was with me when we went to Stockholm and met with [UEFA president] Lennart Johansson, whom I also met in Paris before the World Cup draw. On both occasions, Johansson told me Europe collectively thought it was a mistake to lock Australia and the other nations into the backwater of Oceania. The real complaint for us was not so much getting into Asia—I think that's important to clarify. It was not being away in the backwater of Oceania.

'We got beaten so thoroughly because FIFA was dealing with bigger fish. FIFA had behind the scenes negotiated a complete global reconstitution to account for the demise of the Soviet Union, and managed to massage a consensus. FIFA had to account for 16 new countries coming in. Ten went into Europe. Six went into Asia. Australia was a sideshow—it was only important to us. FIFA really didn't care. In fact, they were irritated that I'd made an issue of it, that we even had a debate on it. The "debate" was really me and about two or three of the Asian countries that Dempsey got to speak against it, and they just took the vote. Everybody was irritated that the "global solution" was being held up for 30 minutes so Australia could whinge about Oceania. Everybody was in on the global fix. It was a show of cards.'

Sitting down the front of the cavernous auditorium, Hill and his entourage, like crabs on a sandbar against an encroaching sea, moved the amendment.

'You have your national name in front of you. When they said, "All those in favour of the amendment," [then-Soccer Australia commissioner] George Negus held up the placard. We looked around, but couldn't see any other placards going with us. Johansson didn't deliver. But about 30 abstained.'

Later, with Hill gone, Scarsella, who'd witnessed Australia's humiliation first-hand in Zurich, steered a different route, resigning his post as chairman of Soccer Australia to replace Dempsey as OFC president. His strategy was to keep Oceania onside and try to press FIFA from within for direct qualification—a high-stakes ploy that came off, albeit briefly.

'I succeeded for six months, when I was on the FIFA executive, to get one spot,' said Scarsella, 'until it was reversed.'

Hill, however, who fell out with Scarsella after he made the switch to the OFC, is having none of it. In his view, his old deputy's gambit was the height of naivete or, as he put it, 'all bullshit'.

'Direct qualification was always a nonsense. It meant we had to take a half-spot from some other confederation. It was never on. Scarsella didn't have a decision in his favour for six months. He had [FIFA president] Sepp Blatter. Blatter is a very cunning operator and was quite happy to make that announcement when it wasn't in his power to do so. It's a decision of the FIFA executive and not Blatter. Blatter knew he could placate all of the Oceania countries and be sure of their ongoing support and comfortably get rolled by the executive. You notice Blatter didn't protest and didn't work to prevent the executive rolling it? Scarsella had an announcement, not a decision.'

Hill was proven right. When the South Americans realised they had effectively lost a World Cup spot—its gimme playoff against Oceania—the whole proposal collapsed spectacularly. Scarsella's grand plan had become a grand folly and Australia was right back where it had started: royally stuck in the middle of nowhere.

'Basically I thought that was the cue for me to walk away from FIFA and the game,' reflected Scarsella. 'I had worked two years to get to that point. I felt absolutely betrayed. It was politics more than what's good for the game—which is FIFA's motto—that really ruled the day.'

The FFA's multibillionaire boss was thus by no means the first person to pursue the idea of Asia. It was getting anyone to take notice of those grovelling pleas that was his great breakthrough.

When in 2003 Lowy had pledged to do his bit to save local football from extinction, he wasted little time before mentioning Asia as a very real possibility for the Socceroos to get to the World Cup. But at that time Lowy was talking about qualifying via a round-robin playoff in Asia after qualifying through Oceania. By the end of 2004, however, with John O'Neill ensconced as his CEO, that goal had changed to becoming part of Asia—without Oceania. In December that year, in the first of many so-called 'football diplomacy' engagements, Lowy and O'Neill flew to Malaysia to meet Mohamed bin Hammam Al-Abdullah, the smooth-talking, smooth-tailored president of the AFC.

For a man with such a high profile—outside of Osama bin Laden, he is arguably the most recognised Arab in Asia—very little is known about Bin Hammam's personal life. He played football as a kid in the Qatari capital, Doha, but as an adult he was forced to make a difficult decision.

'When I became 17, in those days we were regarded as mature enough to get married,' he told me from AFC House in Kuala Lumpur. 'The family made me choose either to get married or play football. I could not have them both, football and a wife. I said, "No. I want to get married and quit football."'

Bin Hammam went into business but stayed involved in football, becoming president of a club called Al Rayyan at the age of 20. He went on to chair the Qatar Football Association and joined the AFC in 1986. Ten years later, he took a seat on FIFA's executive committee. In 2002, he replaced Sultan Ahmad Shah as president and, by diminishing much of his general secretary's responsibilities, became the most powerful man in Asian football.

So powerful in fact, that many observers of the game have him pegged as the next president of FIFA. In *Foul!,* the British journalist Andrew Jennings credits the 'seriously rich' Qatari with being a kingmaker for Blatter and one of the few individuals with the political clout to be able to unseat him: 'In time he might threaten the president. Bin Hammam had helped put Blatter up there and in time, Bin Hammam might take Blatter down.'

But when I asked Bin Hammam whether he had ambitions to take on a higher-level position in world football's governing body, he batted away the question with exquisite diplomacy.

'For the time being I am a member of FIFA,' he smiled. 'I think I'm enjoying my work so far.'

How was it then, that Frank Lowy, a man from a very different circle of influence and cultural background, managed to get Bin Hammam's ear? Lowy is Jewish and is a significant donor to Israeli state institutions. Bin Hammam is a Muslim and is a member of Qatar's Advisory Council, whose ruler, Emir Hamad bin Khalifa Al-Thani, provides funding to the Palestinian group Hamas. As bedfellows, they are as strange as they come.

Power, wherever it comes from, talks in football. There had been meetings between the AFC and the FFA before, but their chinwag that December was the first time the two billionaires had been brought together in the one room.

It soon turned into a budding friendship which then transformed into a symbolic bond when Bin Hammam flew out to Sydney for the Iraq and Indonesia friendlies in March 2005. While in Australia he met the Prime Minister and spent time with Lowy on his floating gin palace, *Ilona IV*, on Sydney Harbour. Just a few weeks later, Australia's move to Asia had been approved in principle and Oceania would not stand in its way—on one important condition. The OFC agreed to the switch as long as FIFA ensured it kept its half-spot in World Cup qualifying (a caveat sweetened considerably a year later when FIFA's executive committee announced that the half-spot playoff would be decided in Asia and not South America). By September, it was official. Australia had become the 46th member of the AFC.

At the time, the event passed with barely a mention in the mainstream news media, but those within the game appreciated its importance. On the first day of 2006, the Socceroos and all its associated national teams would begin playing national and club comps in Asia, including qualifiers for the next World Cup and the fledgling Asian Champions League. It was a long, *long* way, both literally and metaphorically, from the three-men-and-a-magpie days of the National Soccer League.

Tt was only because of Frank,' laughed Bin Hammam when I put it to him that Australia's acceptance by the AFC seemed to catch everyone in the football world by surprise. 'He was the driving force. Before Frank, I never opened the subject of Australia with anybody. There were some discussions before [I was elected president], but it very much goes back to the 1970s and '80s when I wasn't involved at all in football administration in Asia.'

'Was he pushy, persistent?'

'He was convincing.'

Lowy's famous persuasiveness aside, though, what benefit was the AFC getting out of the deal? What had changed since the first calamitous overtures of Sir Arthur George to precipitate such a backflip? After all, the decision had come before the Socceroos had qualified for the World Cup. They'd been slaughtered at the Confederations Cup. John Aloisi hadn't made *that* kick.

'Lowy has shown the value of money. If he didn't get that $15 million from the government we wouldn't have got Guus Hiddink,' said George, a man whose fierce battles with Lowy in the early days of the NSL were the stuff of legend. 'He's wealthy, he has the time, he has a passion for the game and he doesn't like losing. In my opinion he revolutionised the game. Now Bin Hammam is a very, very broadminded internationalist. He realised the AFC were only getting four-and-a-half places at the World Cup. If Australia joined them, they'd get five. He realised eventually Australia would be part of an Asia where we would help to build some of the teams that we would be playing against. Just as they would help us. His interest was to steal from Oceania the best country and the only country that has that ability.'

'FIFA had a problem with Australia they had to resolve,' contended Scarsella. 'The easiest way to resolve it was to take Australia out of Oceania and put it into Asia. So I think it was a combination of two things: Lowy's influential presence as chairman of the Australian FA, and I know for a fact that Blatter felt he owed Australia something for our support in 1998 and 2002.'

Hill agreed: 'It is a fantastic achievement, whoever is responsible. It could not have happened except that FIFA got the AFC to cop it.'

The two men that matter, however, give none of these theories any credence.

'I've never heard any of this,' said Bin Hammam. 'The request from Australia to join Asia, I welcomed the idea. First of all, the way I understood the discussion, Australia didn't have competitive partners [in the OFC]. This was a fact. The Oceania representatives in FIFA competitions were always Australia. It was just like they were playing alone. And of course if you add the commercial value to the Australian federation, it must be much more [to them].

'Frank and I went jointly to Mr Blatter, the FIFA executive committee, and told them Australia wanted to join Asia and to quit Oceania. They said, "Okay, follow the procedures." This wasn't the first time [a country had defected]; Guam also was part of the OFC and joined us.'

Simple as that! Nor was there opposition from within the AFC, even among the traditional anti-Australian factions.

'We are sport people. We separate ourselves from political things. One of my vice-presidents on the executive committee of Asia was absolutely supportive when we proposed the application of Australia. I never really heard any negative comments from any Malaysian, and never read anything negative.'

'We had similar objectives,' said Lowy. 'Bin Hammam wanted us in there and we wanted to be there. It took a lot of negotiations and discussions for us to get into Asia, with the Asian teams, with FIFA—they had a very big say—then Oceania had to let us go, Asia had to take us in, FIFA had to sanction it. There were a lot of people involved, it took quite extensive negotiations, but it was done quite quickly.'

Was he surprised, though, at just how quickly it happened?

'I'm very impatient,' he laughed. 'Everything that happens I want it to happen quickly.'

CHAPTER EIGHT · THE DRILLING FIELDS

'Australian coach Tiko Jelisavcic and co-manager Jim Bayutti, in civilian clothes, went to the stadium to mingle with crowds watching the North Koreans practise. But Cambodian officials guided them to special chairs in the main grandstand, ten yards from the North Korean officials. After the two groups had exchanged side glances for 20 minutes, the Australians introduced themselves. Jelisavcic, after watching the Koreans, said: "We shall beat them."'

AN EXCERPT FROM AN AAP REPORT BY JIM SHRIMPTON IN SYDNEY'S *TELEGRAPH*, 17 NOVEMBER 1965, FILED JUST BEFORE AUSTRALIA'S FIRST EVER WORLD CUP MATCH

Long before the FFA's official embrace by the AFC, Australian players had been forging their own, more personal, ties with our northern neighbours, extending what was left of their careers or making small fortunes in the far-flung reaches of the continent, from the cashed-up oil leagues of the Middle East to the space-age stadia of Japan, and some drained rice paddies in between.

It's a historical footnote, but Australia's national football team first met an Asian side way back in 1923, when a touring Chinese Universities team played a program of five matches around the country, winning just one. Five years later, Australia toured the Dutch East Indies, winning all but five of 23 matches against provincial selections. In 1938, the first Asian-Australian international took place when India played a series of games on the eastern seaboard. The 'Barefoot Indians', as they were called—the majority of the team chose not to wear boots—matched the Aussies in five high-scoring games, losing all but one: they upset the hosts 1-4 in Newcastle. Of the shock win, *The Sun* reported unflatteringly: 'At times, India gave Australia lessons in ball control, tactics and accurate passing.'

It wasn't a fluke. India qualified for the World Cup in 1950 but pulled out because FIFA wouldn't allow them to play barefoot, a decision Indian fans have rued ever since. By 1956, however, most of the team had cottoned on to the benefits of footwear and they returned to Australia for the Melbourne Olympics, where India again faced off against the home side. The Aussies were all over the shop, a Goan player called Neville D'Souza scoring a hat-trick for the Indians in a 4-2 romp.

My friend from Öhringen, Ted Smith, played outside left in that match. He believed the Australians had no one to blame but themselves, even though the squad hardly represented the best available football talent of the time. Players had been picked according to vested political interests, each state being represented in the team.

'It's become folklore that a few of the Indian players took their boots off and that was the reason we didn't feel we could tackle them. But I don't buy that,' he told me. 'They caught us early. They were very quick. We went collectively into the game thinking we were going through. We should have beaten them, and would have been in a semi-final. Not that we would have gone any further, but for the game—which was tiny at that particular time—it would have been massive. You get a shot and you take it. That was the first real world tournament Australia had been in, and I don't think that got through to us either. Before this last World Cup in Germany, someone said that the Socceroos weren't just going there to take part. I think the '56 team felt, "We're at the Olympics" and that was it. It wasn't the start of the destination, it was the end.'

When the embarrassed Aussies complained the win was no reflection of their respective powers, another match was organised, this time in Sydney and without Smith in the line-up. There could be no grumbling after it was over: the Indians won 7-1.

In 1965, after seven years in the international wilderness as a non-FIFA-aligned nation, Australia played its first World Cup qualifying campaign, also in Asia, under the late Tiko Jelisavcic, a one-time Partizan Belgrade striker who migrated to Sydney to coach the Bondi-based club Hakoah Eastern Suburbs. His old friend Rale Rasic described him as 'a beautiful human being, one of the smartest people I ever came across.' However, the players who served under him in the national team held a different view.

Australia was in the unique position of only having to beat North Korea to secure a berth at England '66. South Korea and a raft of African states had pulled out of qualifying for various reasons—unhappiness with only one spot for the Asian and African confederations, financial exigencies and opposition to the inclusion of South Africa, then at the height of its apartheid madness—but the ASF and Kim il-Sung were not bothered by such trifles. As Australia and North Korea did not have diplomatic relations, they agreed to meet in Phnom Penh, Cambodia, for a two-game playoff.

As little as we know about North Korea today, in 1965 its football team may as well have been aliens, such was Australia's knowledge of its opponent. When I asked the team's captain, Les Scheinflug, what he knew about the Koreans, he responded succinctly: 'Zilch.' In front of 60,000 Cambodians, the green Aussies were about to get the shock of their lives.

'We prepared ourselves in Cairns for four weeks because we heard it was hot in Cambodia,' said Scheinflug. 'All we did was train. Train in the morning. Train in the afternoon in the heat. No warm-up games except one match in Ingham. We played one match there and beat a Herbert River select XI 18-0. We had a barbecue after and that's the only thing we did in four weeks.'

Confined to a barracks-like hostel, there was very little to do but play cards, read books and hang out by the pool. Jelisavcic had laid down a strict policy of no drinking, no sex and no skylarking, but conspicuously exempted himself, bringing into camp his wife Seka ...

'She was gorgeous. Absolutely out of this world,' laughed Stan Ackerley, the ex-Manchester United reserve and Australian defender who went on to be a part of the unsuccessful 1969 World Cup qualifying campaign. 'You had all these blokes on heat, and she used to walk around in these little cut-off shorts like girls wear these days. She'd walk down to the pool in a little bikini and we were like, "What's going on here?" We were barred from having a drink, barred from this, barred from that. You looked at her and she was 9 out of 10. Some days she was 11 out of 10.'

John Watkiss, for his part, tried to be professional about it.

'I never really noticed,' he said, deadpan. 'Yeah, she had a good figure. It was distracting, I suppose, especially under the circumstances.'

It was all the more galling for the players because when the team stopped over for a day in Bangkok and got an opportunity to cut loose, Jelisavcic threatened to send home anyone who got intimate with a local girl. But hypocrisy wasn't Jelisavcic's worst trait. It was his habit of cheating at cards. When he was finally caught taking cards from the bottom of the pack, some of the senior players were rightfully incensed. Co-managers Jim Bayutti and Ian Brusasco called a team meeting and, because there was no real option but to continue the tour, it was decided to sweep the matter under the carpet. However, putting their undying faith in the coach was now more difficult and it was a miracle they managed to get to Asia at all.

'Tiko was a very ordinary coach but then to find him cheating his players at cards was too much,' said Brusasco. 'There was a lot of tension on that tour. He didn't have the confidence of the players. But what else could we do?'

'Seven days before the match we went to Cambodia,' said Scheinflug. 'We ate the local food and drank the local water and seven of us had diarrhoea because we didn't know how to prepare. We didn't know North Korea was together for two years as an army team. They prepared themselves exceptionally well. We had no idea about food intake, how to train properly, how to get there, how long before you should go to Phnom Penh, when you should train, how long you should train.'

Tn those days, anything you ate, you just turned around and threw it back up,' said John Roberts, the team's number one. 'I was playing then at about 12 stone and I think I lost a stone and a half by the time I left. I was sharing with Watkiss and it was a fight to see who could commandeer the toilet the whole time. We had the best of food but we just couldn't keep it down. We lived on Green Spot Orange and Coca-Cola.'

When they weren't clenching their sphincters in their rooms at the Hotel Le Royale, the Aussies were further lulled into torpor by the lavish reception their Cambodian hosts put on for them. As *The Sun* reported, they were 'being treated like kings', with all sorts of honours bestowed upon them—the freedom of the city, a 'royal progress' tour through Phnom Penh's streets in the team bus, a full civic reception from the governor with all the bells and whistles. When the two teams met at the palace of Prince Norodom Sihanouk for an official dinner and a performance of the Royal Corps de Ballet, the Koreans—well drilled, focused and continent—were thinking only of the upcoming qualifiers.

Our boys were trying to figure out what was on their plates.

'I'm sitting there, and they brought out 18 courses,' laughed winger Hammy McMeechan, his Glaswegian accent strong even after four decades of living in Australia. 'Long bowls with things in them. I'm waiting for something I recognise before I'm going to eat it, you know. Billy Rorke and Billy Cook were eating everything and anything. A servant brought this jelly thing out, and I said, "Excuse me, do you speak English?" She said yes and told me what it was. When I told the boys, Billy Cook—aw, *ttthhhpppt*—he was spitting his out, and he told Billy Rorke: "That's snake we're eating!" Billy Rorke said: "Is it? You don't want yours then?"'

Scheinflug was the only Australian to score in the two matches, the first a 6-1 hammering, then a more respectable but no less exasperating 3-1 in the reprise, in which Jelisavcic stacked the defence. As Lou Gautier, a writer for Sydney's *Soccer World* newspaper and now a researcher for SBS, wrote prophetically: 'English critics need not worry any more about Australia ruining their fun at the World Cup ... this North Korea will be a tough customer and will be anything but outclassed.'

'They were very, *very* fit,' said Scheinflug. 'Seven of our players from the first team were still down with diarrhoea. We were absolutely shot to bits, gone, out of the world, tired. We had a training session at seven o'clock but couldn't get out of bed until about ten. They were fitter than us, they were sharper on the ball and quite skilful. We had enough skill but our fitness let us down and our lack of competitive matches. With the right preparation we could have been in England, we could have beaten Italy.'

'Before the game we went and watched the Koreans at training,' recalled midfielder Archie Blue. 'They were playing nine a side, taking it easy. What we bloody well did, because we only had a squad of 20, was get two Cambodian players to play with us and have full-scale practice matches two nights before the game. Jelisavcic hadn't even picked his squad! Everybody's running around like a hairy goat because we all wanted to play.'

In the second game, with five goals against and their chances of qualification as good as dead, the Australians could have opted to surrender meekly and be slaughtered by the Koreans, but they gave it their all, refusing to countenance defeat until the final whistle.

'Everybody gave everything they had in that game,' said Watkiss. 'It was very hot, very humid, very draining and [centre-half] Billy Rice collapsed after the game. A couple of the guys picked him up and carried him off on their shoulders to the side of the pitch, and Tiko's reaction was to stand up and say, "Let the bastard walk!" Some of the players flew into him and he lost *all* respect after that.'

Lacking unity and dispirited, the squad eked out a scoreless draw with Cambodia a few days later, then left for Hong Kong, where they took in the sights, learned to use chopsticks, and played a mini-tournament against the hosts, Nationalist China (in reality a Hong Kong FA selection featuring nine Taiwan players) and Swedish club side AIK Stockholm.

In an ill-tempered match against the Taiwanese, which the *China Mail* was moved to call 'a degrading, disgusting, despicable so-called soccer spectacle', the Australians won 3-1 via a Blue hat-trick. But the ugliest scenes were to come after the final whistle. Because the as-then-winless Aussies had been expected to lose, they were heckled as they came off the field and inside the sheds by mobs of aggrieved punters. The fans' mood hadn't been helped when centre-half Cook was sent off for kicking a Taiwan player in the bum. As things rapidly got out of hand, English referee Fred Pratlett told the Australian: 'Son, I'm going to send you off for your own good.'

'When they stormed our dressing-room we were terrified,' said Brusasco. 'We were heavily armed with a bottle of Coke each. I've never been so happy to see riot police.'

Jim Shrimpton, who covered the tour, remembered being in a room upstairs from the sheds, 'phoning my story back to Sydney from underneath a table, because they were throwing rocks through the windows'.

The team was driven back to their hotel in a police van and kept their team blazers hidden in their luggage for the remainder of their stay in the colony. A two-game series in Malaysia followed, the Australians winning both games against the national team convincingly—but their match fitness had kicked in at the wrong end of the tour. When they touched down at Kingsford Smith Airport, Australian football's first foray into Asia—one everyone on the team was already trying to forget—was over. The papers, though, weren't letting up. As Andrew Dettre wrote in *Soccer in Australia:* 'Many critics, especially those not very closely associated with the game, were all too keen to cremate Australian soccer and scatter the ashes into unannounced directions.'

Despite their abject performances, there was brief talk after the tour that Australia would go on to compete in a biennial Interport Cup with Hong Kong and Singapore. Bayutti, showing remarkable foresight, even suggested a regular Asian tournament for teams such as Japan, Taiwan, Cambodia and Australia, with a trophy donated by Prince Sihanouk. Yet, like most ideas well before their time, neither materialised and their proponents would be forgotten, just like Jelisavcic. Within two years of returning to Australia, the coach-cum-card shark had quit his job with Hakoah, sold his unit in Randwick, and decamped with the voluptuous Seka to Africa. They would never return.

Two years later, under new manager Joe Vlasits, an altogether different national team with the ungainly nickname of the 'Socceroos' was invited to return to Indochina, this time to play in the eight-team Vietnam National Day tournament in Saigon. It would be Australia's first outing in a multi-team tournament in Asia and, on its conclusion, its first trophy in senior men's international football. But there was more at stake than winning a few football matches. 'It wasn't until years later that I realised how the team had been blindly steered into helping the war effort,' wrote team captain Johnny Warren in his autobiography, *Sheilas, Wogs & Poofters.*

The disaster in Phnom Penh had taught the team some valuable lessons—most importantly, to never underestimate their opponents—but nothing could have prepared them for the psychological challenge of playing in the midst of a war. Pride in the shirt wouldn't stop a landmine going off beneath their feet.

'We were playing in a war zone,' recollected striker Ray Baartz. 'There was talk that security had actually caught some Viet Cong trying to blow up the hotel. We weren't aware of that until much later on. We had army and police protection to and from a game, with the sirens blaring. Everyone got out of the way whenever we went anywhere. You'd go to the stadium and soldiers would be going around the ground with mine detectors. It was quite unnerving. Then there was the oppressive heat, monsoon conditions, the grounds were caked in mud, and when you're not eating and drinking it's hard to put in 110 per cent. But we rose to the occasion and, if anything, it did bond us.'

Ackerley remembered it as a terrifying experience: 'We played South Vietnam; there were riots because we were giving them a good hiding. The Asians are quite big gamblers, even when there's a war going on, and they went to town on us. It was frightening. We were young and silly. When I look back on it, I think we were bloody idiots going there.'

It was just as dangerous inside the players' hotel rooms at the deceptively named Golden Building.

'My god, my *god,*' laughed Atti Abonyi. 'It was by far the worst place anyone could have gone to in 1967. Honestly, I'm not kidding you. Being in Vietnam was a bloody eye-opening experience at the time anyway. The conditions, the poverty. Everything was just absolutely shithouse. The most terrible place you could ever go to.'

This was something Ackerley would soon discover first-hand—literally.

'We checked in, I put my case down and opened the bloody door and I put my hand around to put the light on and grabbed a live wire,' he said. 'Next minute I was thrown right across the room. I was semi-conscious, burnt my socks, my arms, my fingers—the electricity went right through my body. If it wasn't for [team doctor] Brian Corrigan working on me, I would have been in a bloody bad way.'

In another room, German-born defender Manfred Schaefer, who would make his international debut in Saigon against New Zealand, was sharing with Warren and goalkeeper Roger Romanowicz.

'Johnny was the most clever of the three of us. He slept next to the shower,' he said. 'We found out later that if you did get attacked, into the shower you'd go.'

The crumbling Golden Building also doubled as a training pitch. With a distinct lack of adequate facilities on offer—one overgrown block they'd practised near was covered in live landmines—the Australians had to be resourceful.

'The hotel had a flat roof,' said Abonyi. 'We used to train up there and the balls used to fall down into the main street. Balls were bouncing everywhere.'

In their time off, the players would nick out, keen to sample as much of the Saigon nightlife as possible. But rather than ease the team's collective anxiety, their nocturnal wanderings only exacerbated it.

'We never went around in less than pairs,' recalled Ackerley. 'We were told to keep out of the bars. There were kids going around with machine guns and blowing places up. All the bars had electric doors. One night I went out with [*Daily Mirror* reporter] Terry Smith and Johnny Watkiss to [Australian army HQ] The Canberra, and we were having a few beers, and sure enough we got carried away in conversation and different things, and all of a sudden the shutters went down and we couldn't get out. We had to get back to the hotel. Eventually we got out and we got a lift on one of these troop carriers, past the Vietnamese "White Mice", past the Korean police, then the American MPs. We were only a couple of blocks away from the Golden Building but you would not dare walk. We were scared. All the boys look back it on it now, though, and we'd do it all again.'

After they'd won the tournament, prevailing 3-2 over South Korea at a packed Cong Hoa Stadium, the Australian air force flew the Socceroos, flushed with success and a few too many beers, in a DHC-4 Caribou airlift carrier down to the Australian military's R&R base at Vũng Tàu, a bustling city on the South China Sea.

'We were flying all over the jungles, and the bloody Caribou, they kept the back of it open the whole way down,' said Baartz, referring to the platform that was usually lowered for parachute drops. 'When we got down to Vũng Tàu, the pilot said, "I'll show you the beach", and he was going 20 feet above the sand, buzzing the beach, so it was a bit of a hairy experience.'

There the team played a kickaround game against a Combined Services XI, winning 8-1, though no one was keeping count. Football was a popular pastime for the men at the base; for months they'd been playing games against the locals on Saturdays, trying to bridge the cultural divide.

'We had a great time,' said Ackerley. 'It was the first chance we'd had to really let loose. We had a massive barbecue. There were all these snakes hanging over the fence. The lads had been in the water, and were catching all these sea snakes on the beach.'

Abonyi agreed: 'It was like a picnic for us. We'd been in Vietnam for two weeks by then. We were so glad to get out of Saigon. It was a hell of a day. The soldiers were so good to us. Drinking, eating. Absolutely brilliant. It didn't really hit us until we came back that "Shit, we've just been in Vietnam!" *Christ.* Who would have thought we'd have gone there?'

After the encouraging performances by Australia at the 1974 World Cup, forward Adrian Alston was the only player to field offers to play abroad. As most of his team-mates had originally fled Britain and Europe in search of better lives and decent incomes, they were in no hurry to go back. But two Australians in Germany at the time had made an altogether different choice—to play their club football in Asia.

Goalkeeper Dennis Boland, who emigrated from Scotland in 1970 and put in a few seasons with Footscray JUST in the NSL, was never in the frame for the national team, but in 1974 he went to the opening game of the World Cup and played a series of friendlies against second-division German and Dutch squads for Japanese club Yomiuri FC. Today, the Yomiuri club is known as Tokyo Verdy 1969, and is one of the most famous clubs in Asia.

Ex-Socceroo Hammy McMeechan accompanied Boland—it was McMeechan, in fact, who'd recommended him to Yomiuri's coach—but in Germany the two men parted company. McMeechan quit the team when the club barred him from bringing his fiancée to Tokyo. Boland, who was already married, went to Japan and would go on to play two seasons in the Japan Soccer League, in 1974/'75 and 1975/'76. So secured his unlikely place in Australian football history.

'Japan was a culture shock but a super experience,' Boland told me from Melbourne, where he now works as a gas pipeline salesman. 'The team was run by the Nippon Television Company, and money was not a factor. Everything was done so professionally: full-time training; they put me and my wife up in a two-storey house; the club gave us tickets to anywhere in the world at the end of the season. Everything was laid on for the players.'

At that time, well before the advent of the J. League, Japanese football was little more than a way for companies to earn bragging rights by attaching their name to a successful sports club. The players were salaried employees of the companies, but weren't expected to do anything outside of training and playing football. As Boland quipped: 'The closest I got to the Nippon Television Company was the TV in the lounge room.'

'It wasn't like the Japan of today. It was very hard to get Australian steak or steak of any sort. And when we travelled away, like when we went to Osaka, we'd have to go on the bullet train or coach and I'd be billeted in a Japanese motel with the team.

That was very different—sitting on the floor, eating what they were eating, wearing kimonos, wandering about the place. That was a real culture shock. Once my wife and I got invited to a neighbour's house for dinner and none of them spoke English. That was pretty hard. His little girl, who was seven, tried to translate everything. Me with a Scottish accent trying to speak Japanese made it very hard for her.'

In the late 1970s and early '80s, a few notables, such as Socceroos Doug Utjesenovic, Terry Butler and Oscar Crino, would follow Boland's lead, playing their off-seasons in Hong Kong. A handful came after, including David Mitchell and Robbie Dunn, but the Aussie invasion of Asian football would reach its peak in the early to mid-'90s, when the likes of Abbas Saad, Mehmet Durakovic, Warren Spink, Scott Ollerenshaw and Alistair Edwards became big names in Malaysia. Perhaps the best known of Australia's exports to Asia of that era is Craig Foster, who pitched up in Singapore as a pink-cheeked teenager to play for the national team in the Malaysian league.

'Edwards and Saad had gone over the year before. These were the days when the NSL was only six months a year,' he said. 'There was no money in Australia. Nor was there security of contracts in the NSL. All of a sudden we started getting offers to go over to Asia for three or four months and get paid good money. It was like, "Christ, we can be professional here." Of course, what I really needed was someone to pull me aside and say, "Don't be stupid, stay in Australia and try to develop yourself," but I was 19 years old. So I went to Singapore and it took me years to get back to the level I was at before. But playing in Asia was an incredible experience. Even in Singapore, they had 70,000 people to every home match.

'I enjoyed the off-field lifestyle far too much. I didn't make the Socceroos till I was 26, principally because I'd played in Asia. The good ones were going to Europe and the middle ones were going over to Asia and earning the sort of living that they couldn't get in Europe anyway. For the guys playing at the top

Malaysian teams, however, the quality was quite good. You'd have players come in from Africa, Croatia and so on, and it was decent standard. Big crowds. Good hype. Very enjoyable. But with the A-League here now, there's no reason to go over anymore.'

He's correct. Today, with good money and a decent league on offer at home, and with second-tier footballers heading to Eastern Europe, only half a dozen Australians turn out in the Malaysian league; retired Socceroo Tony Popovic, who spent his best years in Japan, is our sole representative in the Middle East, with Qatari club Al Arabi. In South-East Asia, the former hub of Australian expat footballers in the east, salaries have slumped from their pre-economic crisis highs; African footballers, who are often prepared to work for less than their European counterparts, are flooding the market. In Singapore, three or four years ago, a good Australian footballer could command about $8000 a month plus bonuses. Now they're lucky to get half that.

AFC president Mohamed bin Hammam is convinced the biggest opportunities for Australians in Asian football now lie not in playing but in coaching, citing Asia's poor training infrastructure and Australia's comparative riches. Part of the trail has already been cleared. West Australians such as two-time Melbourne Knights coach Ken Worden and former Perth Glory coach Alan Vest have both enjoyed success in Malaysia; ex-Matildas coach Steve Darby is currently employed at Perak in Ipoh and had a stint helming the Vietnamese women's team; and in October 2006, Dusan Purac, a Sydney-based junior skills coach, was lured to Saudi Arabia to start an academy for Saudi youth, making him Australia's highest paid football coach. For those who are prepared to brave the hot weather and a little bit of cultural adjustment, the opportunities are boundless.

'Australia can really help our national associations with your coaches, or we could send our top coaches in Asia to be educated there, definitely,' said Bin Hammam. 'That is one thing we at the AFC think about. With Australia joining Asia, passion for football in Australia must be going to increase both in the short term and long term. Long term, it depends on the Australian league being one of the best in the world in the future. This is the target and the aim of the AFC—to compete with European football. So far, our aim is to be second to Europe. But with time we should provide the talent with the chance to choose between Asia and Europe. That's the dream we have.

'Australia can have a lot of influence on [Asian] football and Asian football can have a positive influence and improve the standard of football in Australia. We can do that by making the game much more popular than it used to be and give Australia a better platform for competitive matches and direction between administrators, clubs and leaders. These sort of "experience exchanges" Australia needed very much.

'Asia is benefiting from the professionalism of the Australian administration. We are lacking that in this part of the world, and we want to develop our football to have a profile in international football. We need professionalism and professional minds.'

In Asia, though, professionalism cannot solve all footballing problems. Take the case of Scott O'Donell, a journeyman footballer who left the NSL's Parramatta Eagles for Malaysia in the mid-1990s. In 2003, armed with an Australian coaching licence, he took the reins of Singapore team Geylang United and led them to the championship final. That season he was named S. League Coach of the Year. Through pure happenstance, while O'Donell and his wife were in the process of adopting two orphaned girls in Phnom Penh, Prince Norodom Ranariddh offered him the coaching job of Cambodia, regarded as the worst team in Asia. No one, not even the FFA, knew Australia had its first coach of a foreign national football team. Even O'Donell's old mentor, former Socceroos coach Raul Blanco, was in the dark.

Within six months, though, just as his squad was about to depart for the Southeast Asian Games, O'Donell's plans fell in a heap. The prince, in his erstwhile role as National Olympic Committee boss, had on a whim decided he wanted to replace the entire national squad with the country's leading club side, which he just happened to own and had a bad habit of coaching unofficially from the stands. O'Donell was given the new toothless title of technical director.

'My wife Margaret had just resigned from her job and the kids were moving up here from Singapore,' he told me. 'We moved a containerload of all our belongings to Phnom Penh. So I was in a kind of situation where if she hadn't resigned and the kids hadn't moved up I would've left and gone back to Singapore. It was just a complete fuck-up but I had to make the best of it.'

So for eight months O'Donell bided his time watching training sessions and writing reports, and waited for the unique mechanics of Cambodian politics to sort out the mess. Prime Minister Hun Sen barred Ranarridh from having anything to do with the national team and called a snap election of the Cambodian Football Federation (CFF), which saw the CFF president replaced by the head of the military police. But when FIFA threatened to suspend the country from world football for political meddling, O'Donell got his old job back and order was restored.

So what advice does O'Donell have for Australian coaches contemplating a move to Asia?

'Lower your expectations. If you're used to working with national league-standard players, one thing you can't expect is all the players you're working with to be up to that standard, or even the level of professionalism. One of the things I had to do in Singapore and also in Cambodia was to try to get the players to understand what it meant to be professional, to live a professional life. Like in terms of nutrition, looking after injuries, just doing the basics. In Australia, when I was in the NSL, everyone knew what to do, knew how to look after themselves. So the education process is important.

'But also they have to be aware of the culture they're working in. If you're working with Muslims, you've got to understand that during fasting month you can't push the players as hard. Just little things. A lot of it is common sense. Don't compromise your principles, because I would never do that in terms of how I want teams to play or pushing players, but you have to appreciate the culture and try to adapt to it the best you can without compromising yourself.'

O'Donell admits he's one of the luckiest Australian coaches working anywhere in the world.

'You look at all the good coaches in Australia who are out of jobs at the moment, and I'm doing something I love doing, I'm getting paid for it, I'm full time. I wouldn't have that opportunity in Australia. I'd love to go home and spend time with my mum and dad, brothers and sisters, nieces and nephews, but in terms of the opportunities I have here, I don't have that back in Australia. There, my profile is basically zero. I was just an average player in the NSL. At the time I played we hardly got any media exposure at all. I was a teacher.

'Sure, Cambodia is different, the first six months were tough, but I enjoy living up here. It's a lot more relaxed than Singapore, or even Sydney for that matter. It made it a lot easier having lived in Asia for ten years—if I had come straight from Australia I probably would have got more of a culture shock—but coming here every year since we adopted the kids made things easy.'

The Stade Olympique, the same arena where Tiko Jelisavcic's Australians played their hearts out in the heat of a tropical November night four decades ago, still stands today. Then it was just a year old, an awe-inspiring piece of architecture, a marvel even to the first-world Australians. Now it is a decaying shell, its electricity and sewerage systems so inadequate that Cambodia lost its right to host the 2004 Tiger Cup (now the ASEAN Cup) over the issue. But it's in good enough condition to be used by O'Donell and his struggling Cambodia team. They have little choice in the matter. It's the only decent ground in the country.

In the clumpy grass under O'Donell's feet, where he takes his wide-eyed men through physical and technical sessions six times a week, lie the tread marks of Billy Rice and the '65 Socceroos. Here, in this forgotten field in South-East Asia, not Germany, is where the real legend of the Socceroos was born.

CHAPTER NINE · THE BAD COP

'Time is an awkward inconvenience between football matches.'

ALBERT CAMUS

Germany 2006 was not a good tournament for Asian teams, yet the fact that all four of the AFC's entrants (bar Australia, which qualified through Oceania) were eliminated in the first round is deceptive. Like the Socceroos, Japan drew with Croatia and even scored against Brazil—something Australia could not—in their last group game before being steamrolled. South Korea won its first World Cup match on foreign soil and held France to a 1-1 draw. Saudi Arabia nabbed its first ever World Cup point against Tunisia and lost narrowly to Spain. Only Iran, a traditional AFC heavyweight, could be said to have had a poor all-round showing, being hammered by Mexico and Portugal and only managing a draw with Angola.

So the Asian teams are hardly pushovers. Certainly they presented a greater threat to Australia's Asian Cup hopes than the FFA appeared to believe: just four weeks after the World Cup, it made public what many observers had suspected for months: that no viable 'first-tier' coaching replacement for Guus Hiddink had been found. The Dutchman, freshly minted with a new dye job for his whitening locks, could have been forgiven for thinking he'd been rash in defecting to Russia. Where Australia had been grateful for this much-starred foreigner to come in and save their bacon, the Russians were up in arms, complaining that Hiddink didn't understand the Russian soul.

Graham Arnold understood the Australian soul, all right; his credentials as an all-round top Aussie bloke could not be doubted. It was his CV as a coach that undermined whatever claim he had to permanently replace Hiddink. But for now, until after the Asian Cup finals in July 2007, the FFA made it clear that Arnold would do.

For an organisation that had set so many new benchmarks for the local game, the decision to back Arnold on an 'interim' basis was a big comedown for the fans. They'd expected the FFA to capitalise on the goodwill to the sport that had been generated by the Socceroos at the World Cup. Getting into Asia had been promoted as the FFA's biggest achievement, even more than World Cup qualification, but now Australia was about embark on its next football mission half-cocked, led by a less-than-world-class coach and carrying that 'she'll be right' mentality that had got them into so much trouble in the past.

John O'Neill, possibly mindful of the growing perception in the media that all wasn't wine and roses at College Street, was careful to use the rider 'Frank and I' when telling the press that Arnold didn't have the FFA's support beyond the final in Jakarta on 29 July 2007. Never mind that Arnold, his assistant John Kosmina and closely aligned journalists were claiming that he was ready to take Australia to South Africa 2010. Kosmina even went so far as to retract comments he'd made in 2005 that no local coach was up to the task. But O'Neill was firm: when there was a 'calmer environment' after the Asian tournament, the decision to find a Mr Big of world football would be made. Such a delay would also allow names such as Hiddink and the elusive Gérard Houllier to re-enter the equation for 2010, as both would be coming off contract.

Despite his disappointment at not securing a long-term position, this was still an opportunity for Arnold, who'd rejected an offer to coach his old club in Holland, Roda JC Kerkrade. A player who'd never quite reached giddy heights for either club or country, Arnold had followed Frank Farina and Robbie

Slater to Europe in the late 1980s and saw out several successful seasons in the Dutch Eredivisie before returning to Australia to fulfil the player-coach role with Northern Spirit in the dying days of the NSL. His coaching was a mixed bag, Spirit making the finals in 1998 but finishing a poor 13th the following year. This, however, was not enough to deter his old mate Farina from picking Arnold as his assistant when he was appointed Socceroos coach in 2000.

As assistant to Hiddink, Arnold had got his first taste of managing an international side when he stepped in as caretaker for an AFC qualifier in Bahrain in February 2006, the Socceroos' first match in their new confederation. A team containing a mix of experienced rep players and young bolters looking to stake last-minute claims for Hiddink's Germany squad finished over the top of their opponents 3-1, an adequate though unspectacular debut against very average opposition, but it was hard to draw any conclusions about Arnold's coaching from this one hit-out. Only when the shadow of Hiddink had fully lifted could more reasoned judgments be made.

His audition would come quickly enough with two home-and-away Asian Cup qualifiers against Kuwait in August, the Socceroos' first games since being knocked out in Kaiserslautern. Kuwait wasn't exactly a top-shelf team, but had enough pedigree to prevent Australia having the run of the field. Nevertheless, the timing of the games presented a problem for the new coach. With the World Cup over and the European club season in full swing, changes to the side were inevitable. Australian fans would be cheering a far different side from the one that had enchanted the world a month before.

Just how different was immediately apparent from Arnold's choice of captain, Melbourne Victory's Kevin Muscat. One of the A-League's 'returned Roos', Muscat was old-school, a tough-guy defender who'd left a deep impression at notorious London club Millwall and was known as the 'most hated man' in English football. His antics put many players on stretchers and even landed him in court when he was sued for $6 million for a tackle on Charlton midfielder Matthew Holmes that was so hard doctors feared they'd have to amputate a leg. Back home as a midfield general for Victory, Muscat had carried on pretty much as he'd left off.

Though a regular in the national team under Farina, Muscat hadn't got a guernsey under Hiddink and had been frozen out ever since. So his selection, albeit in a side that had only Mark Milligan and Archie Thompson backing up from the World Cup squad, wasn't much of a statement about the freshness of the approach Arnold was taking into this new era for the Socceroos, a period when so much was at stake for the team as a 'brand' following the World Cup.

However, the sport, as the FFA well knew, was enjoying a honeymoon period where the merest whiff of dissent or cynicism was pounced on as being unpatriotic. Even with a third-string side on offer, the FFA could do no wrong, trotting out the new boys for the standard kickaround in the surf at Bondi Beach—a publicity stunt that continued the timeworn practice of reducing players to performing seals.

Yet something about the completeness of the team's remodelling must have irked the public. Only 32,000 fans turned up at Aussie Stadium when the match had been spruiked as a sellout, and those fans would suffer for their dedication. In the battle of minds with his Kuwait counterpart, Mihai Stoichiţă, Arnold appeared to be out of his depth. He was as animated on the sideline as he had been in Germany, wore the right-coloured suit, acted like a coach, but didn't have the counsel of the calm and experienced Hiddink to call upon to get his team out of what was rapidly turning into a grade-A cockup.

Something about the team seemed amiss, quite apart from the fact that the XI on the park bore no resemblance to the first-choice line-up. Where Hiddink's Australia had played an efficient passing game, building up attacks patiently from deep in their own half, Arnold's version was relying on long balls from the back to neutralise an efficient, committed Kuwaiti midfield that had the ability to get forward but just couldn't make their chances pay. It took nearly half an hour for Australia's first chance on goal, and 75 minutes before the Kuwaiti goalmouth was finally breached. A second goal late in the game rounded out a most unconvincing display.

On paper, the 2-0 scoreline was the standard 'result'. But if this was, as the FFA PR machine wanted us to believe, the all-important first step on the road to 2010, then Australia was going some way backwards, not forwards. Australians had witnessed inventive, skilful, entertaining football from the Socceroos at the World Cup. The encore in Sydney was an abject letdown. As one reader, 'The Clensh', said on my blog on the Fox Sports website: 'I've settled on being able to distinguish between our 2 national football (soccer) teams. When I refer to them, the full-strength team will stay as the "Socceroos" while the ugly stepchild of a team that paraded around last night will be called the "Sh*taroos". Someone please let the [FFA] marketing department know to make the required adjustments to any marketing material for the future.'

What year was this? O'Neill had come into the chief executive's job in 2003 saying he expected Australia's best side out on the park every time, club protestations or not. He'd even made the audacious move to ban Scott Chipperfield and Mark Viduka when they didn't turn up for a friendly in Caracas, Venezuela, in 2004. How to explain, then, the imitation side foisted on the Australian public in 2006? The fans, though, were prepared to let this aberration slide. The return leg in Kuwait City in a few weeks' time would sort out all of Arnold's teething problems.

For this second match, the full World Cup team would again be on ice, though several of the bigger names—John Aloisi, Mark Schwarzer, Chipperfield, Jason Culina—had indicated their willingness to make the trip to the Middle East. None of the players from Sydney would be selected. This new squad would largely be made up of European-based bolters such as Leicester City's central defender Patrick Kisnorbo and Queens Park Rangers midfielder Nick Ward, and some more experienced players who'd been unlucky to miss out on Germany, such as Ahmad Elrich and Ljubo Milicevic.

Yet what transpired, even with seven members of the World Cup squad present, was even more disastrous than Sydney, the result being reversed in the home side's favour. Only one or two genuine chances were created by the Socceroos, the best a gimme for debutant Ryan Griffiths in front of an open goal that ended up smacking off the crossbar. The Kuwaitis, ranked almost 100 in the world, manufactured two technically well-executed goals in open play, their skilful football befitting a much better side.

The stamina-preserving tactics, the volcanic desert heat, the minimal preparation, the loss of backroom staff and even the calling-off of the proposed Lebanon fixture in Adelaide because of the Hezbollah-Israel conflagration were cited as contributing factors to the poor showing in Kuwait. There were grounds, to be fair, for countenancing all of them. But what had Arnold and his employers reasonably expected? Missing, amid all the excuses that were made at the time, was a simple admission that the performance just hadn't been good enough. Arnold fudged: 'It would have been a totally different game if we had scored,' Kuwait 'rose to the occasion ... at the end of the day they had better performance'. Hiddink almost certainly would not have bothered. After Honiara in September 2005, he'd hammered his team: 'If we play again like we did against the Solomon Islands we will have no chance of qualifying [for the World Cup]. We must get to a much higher level.'

Contrition would have been the more appropriate response from Arnold, followed by a long hard look at what he had failed to do to ensure Australia came away with a result, and stating a commitment to eliminate those oversights next time. But nothing of the sort occurred. It was left to his detractors and supporters to thrash it out in the media.

By the end of 2006, a more mature Arnold admitted that his performance in Kuwait had been inadequate.

'I obviously made mistakes,' he told me. 'The biggest was not taking the team that played here in Sydney straight across and keeping them in camp and preparing close by to Kuwait. When I say that was a mistake, that was probably one thing I should have been more forceful on but it was very difficult because there's no FIFA [international] dates in the A-League. I would have been taking 20 players out of the A-League.

'With two days' preparation in those conditions, it can't work. Unless we can get European-based players a week ahead to prepare over there, it's a total waste of time. So, yes, I took a risk here in Sydney, I took a risk in Kuwait. I learned: No more risks. The preparation has to be spot-on; the A-League has to have FIFA dates; tactically I tried to change our method of defending closer to our goal because of the heat but still putting a physical demand on the players, and it's not possible. If anything, I should have probably dropped much deeper in our own half and played four or five at the back and pretty much waited for the counter or the break.'

He'd also reconsidered how he looked on camera. Chewing gum, an old habit, was no longer an option. Hiddink had told him to cut it out.

'He said, "You fucking look like Mr Ed."'

Three weeks after the Kuwait match, another incarnation of the national team—this time Australia's World Cup squad minus the crocked Kewell and Viduka—returned to Australia for a friendly against Paraguay in Brisbane. The game was promoted as a sort of proxy ticker-tape parade, a way of 'saying thanks to the boys' for their showing in Germany and to send off the retiring quartet of Stan Lazaridis, Zeljko Kalac, Tony Vidmar and Tony Popovic. Yet Arnold chose to deviate from the script, using the occasion to reaffirm his candidacy for the top job. He talked about 'drawing a line in the sand' between this match and the

World Cup, saying the Hiddink era was over and he deserved to be seen as a football practitioner in his own right.

Arnold proved he meant business by axeing Craig Moore, one of the team's veterans, for missing a training session. Moore claimed he'd taken a sleeping tablet and this was why he'd missed his flight from Sydney to Brisbane. This wasn't the way intra-team matters had been dealt with in the past. In 2001, after the Socceroos' first-leg World Cup qualifier defeat of Uruguay in Melbourne, cleaners had found 132 empty beer bottles scattered on the hotel-room floor of two senior players. At the time, under Farina, no one was called to account. The proverbial nod-and-a-wink was good enough. Now under Arnold, a man who'd seen how Hiddink kept a tight leash on his players, it was made clear: skylarking would no longer be tolerated.

That was where the similarities between the master and his apprentice ended. When the Socceroos took to the pitch at Suncorp Stadium, it was soon apparent that Arnold's approach owed more to his time under Farina than the storied Hiddink. The team had their first—wayward—shot on goal after half an hour, and made their most incisive run out from the back line, with crisp, low, Hiddink-style passing, with 20 minutes left to play. Arnold's substitutions also betrayed his inexperience. On 72 minutes, he took off Vidmar and replaced him with Jade North—another defender but one out of form—when the scores were tied at nil-all and a goal just didn't look in the offing. Worse, he had two of the most attacking players from the A-League, Travis Dodd and Alex Brosque, still on the bench. Where was the Hiddink-style courage to go for the win?

When the Australian goal eventually came, with minutes left on the clock, it was from a defender, Popovic, heading in from a generously placed free kick. In open play, the Socceroos' forward momentum had been substandard. Brett Emerton was again clamping up when a strike begged, and turning over possession with unnecessary tricks. The committed Paraguayan defence looked unbreakable in the last third of the pitch, and corners, as they had been in Germany, were again so ineffective as to make them almost a write-off from the moment the ball was placed on the spot.

The night may not have proved the celebration of fine attacking football that Arnold and the FFA had hoped for, but at least one man was left impressed by the 55,000-strong sellout. At home watching the game from his lounge chair, Sir Arthur George was seeing football capture the imagination of a sector of the community he never thought could be won over: children, women, the elderly and even fans of the other codes.

'The last time Australia played Paraguay in Brisbane, about 3000 people turned up,' he said.

Four days later, the game's newcomers were out in force again, this time at Aussie Stadium in Sydney's eastern suburbs for the return Asian Cup qualifier against Bahrain. On the train from Strathfield, I'd sat behind a couple from Penrith making their first trip to a football match. Slugging mouthfuls from their cans of UDL, they were discussing their post-game drinking plans. At Central Station, the queue to get on buses taking fans to the stadium was at least 500 metres long. The faces of the fans were new, too. Chinese kids who looked like they'd come straight from chess club. Young fathers with infant daughters. Pairs of good-looking young women wearing yellow scarves and hoop earrings. Two years before, the scene had been very different: I'd travelled to the same ground to see Australia play Turkey, but there'd been more Turkish fans than our own. No matter how the Socceroos were playing right now under Arnold, one thing could not be questioned: as George had intimated, that fortnight in Germany had changed the Australian game forever.

Again, there were moments of finesse and precision from the Socceroos, but something wasn't quite right. The team was still playing Hiddink-style football but the rigid organisation and discipline the Dutchman had instilled were starting to deteriorate. Emerton, Neill and Culina attempted manoeuvres they would never have dared in Germany—perhaps forgivable given the inferior opposition and the siege-like formation of the youthful Bahrainis—but when they didn't come off, holes began appearing in their own defence that were exploited easily on the counterattack. Down the right, especially, a sprite called Ismaeel Hasan was making fools of the Australian backs. Our 2-0 win was hardly the building block for the team's future Arnold had wanted, and did little to quell the calls for his immediate removal as coach, but he remained coolly confident. In his own words, the performance had 'shown that the FFA can relax'.

I'd left the ground early, with a quarter hour to go, and already the shuttle buses were filling up with people, many of them the same faces I'd seen looking so excited and expectant before the game. The mood was funereal, hardly a word spoken. If ever there was confirmation that winning isn't everything in sport, it was being on one of those buses. The Socceroos might have comfortably defeated Bahrain, but how they had won the match had left many unimpressed. The Beautiful Game can sometimes be a very boring one too.

A competitive match had to be organised and pronto. Within a week, the FFA delivered. The Socceroos would meet Germany 2006 surprise packet Ghana in London, almost a year to the day that Hiddink had achieved the impossible dream of a World Cup reprise for Australia.

It would prove an extraordinary, high-tempo game in which the two attacks came at one another with such metronomic force that it made you almost dizzy watching it. The Socceroos were let down by a lousy piece of goalkeeping by Schwarzer and some typical wastefulness up front. Arnold didn't have his best team on the park—Cahill, Kewell, Viduka and Neill were out with injuries—but Ghana coach Claude Le Roy wasn't exactly throwing everything he had at his rival either. He'd been forced to switch the stalwart defensive partnership of Illiasu Shilla and John Mensah for the debut pairing of Eric Addo and Francis Dickoh, and took the unusual step of benching his most prized forward, Udinese's Asamoah Gyan, for rookie Junior Agogo.

So the opportunity was there for Arnold to try something new. Instead, he chose to show he could get the team playing like they did in Germany, keeping play high up the park, with his tried-and-true performers playing to their limits. Only Kisnorbo, in at centre-half for Neill, was a forced substitution, though he proved he was more than capable of holding his own.

Encouragingly, it was Australia's most convincing display since Munich. The interplay and awareness between Sterjovski, Culina, Emerton, Chipperfield and Wilkshire was thrilling to watch. Up until the departure of the peerless Vince Grella early in the second half with a foot injury, the Socceroos' only obstacle to scoring a dozen against arguably Africa's best team was self-belief. The way they were dominating the West Africans confounded all reason. This was not Jamaica. It was *Ghana*.

Yet there remained a thorn in the team's side, one that had never quite gone away: the Socceroos' continued inability to capitalise on free kicks and corners. For a bloke who was setting Serie A alight with Palermo, Mark Bresciano looked decidedly ordinary with the dead ball, one kick sliced into the crowd and 20 metres from the goal. It hadn't even been mishit. Newcastle Jets midfielder Nick Carle, a classic number ten the likes of which Australia has not seen for some time, could be a potential solution in this vexed national-team role—in fact, many within the football community have been quietly pressing for it.

Yet Carle's predicament is symptomatic of the chief failing of the Socceroos post-Germany 2006. There has been too little initiative in making the hard decisions about personnel—forcing retirements, saying no to past-it veterans, bringing in young players, settling on a single 'A-team'—and an overreliance on the tactics that Hiddink brought to the side in the period before and during the World Cup. The new generation of Socceroos in the wings—David Williams, Brad Jones, Danny Vukovic, Scott McDonald, Kaz Patafta, Neil Kilkenny, Nathan Burns, Bruce Djite, Carle and others like them—need to be blooded early and taught these systems inside out, but a surfeit of riches in certain positions and motivations about job security and short-term success are keeping them sidelined.

The story of Carle, a Chilean-Australian product of Sydney's southern districts, is particularly dispiriting when it is plain to anyone who watches him play that he has the technical ability, fitness and, most importantly, youth, to contribute many good years to the senior men's national team. (The A-League's players agreed, paying him the ultimate honour of being voted Johnny Warren Medallist for A-League Player of the Year in February 2007.) But he comes from a culture that still largely values the team over the individual, that remains suspicious of flamboyance or expressiveness in its football. Arnold, for one, wasn't about to offer any succour to Carle's legion of supporters when I spoke to him in late 2006.

'There's plenty of opinion about Nicky and he is having a fine season,' said Arnold. 'Unfortunately he plays in a position where we've got an abundance of top-shelf players—Bresciano, Kewell, Cahill, Culina, Wilkshire, Holman, Grella. So he's behind the eight-ball in that side of it. If you play against a team that's going to stack their defence, Nicky is someone that can come off the bench or be involved, that can break the game open, because he does have good skill.

'Around the box he doesn't score goals from free kicks. I question whether his technique is better than Bresciano from free kicks and corners. Or Skoko or even Chipperfield. The international game is totally different to the A-League. If you saw even the pace of the Ghana game, to get around the field and to be able to play in tight areas and get around that quick is a huge difference to the A-League.'

This is slightly disingenuous and unfair to Carle. If anyone has the ability to create something out of a tight spot, any football fan who knows the Australian game would rate him as the best in the business. And if we are discussing fitness levels, why even mention Skoko at all, given Hiddink froze him out of World Cup planning because of a perceived weakness in that area? Skoko is 31, Carle 25. Younger men have fresher legs. Arnold would know that. So why the conservatism?

Perhaps it doesn't really matter what Carle or any young player does on the park when Arnold's priority, as he readily admitted to me, is not building a likely team for a South Africa 2010 campaign but winning the Asian Cup. This runs counter to the modus operandi of the other big Asian football nations, who primarily use the tournament as a proving ground for the players earmarked for their next World Cup campaigns. This is certainly the strategy being adopted by Australia's two main rivals, Japan and South Korea.

'The Asian Cup is an opportunity for Japan to show its strength and for ourselves to measure how the team is maturing,' the Samurai Blue's new coach, Ivica Osim, told me through an interpreter. 'I am choosing players for the long term. As for results, nothing is impossible in football, which means that even the best team could lose. But at least we can believe our youngsters have more of a future.'

His South Korean counterpart, Dutchman Pim Verbeek, who was assistant to Hiddink at Korea-Japan 2002 and to Dick Advocaat at Germany 2006, is also a strong believer in developing young talent, a position that was reinforced when he saw how South Korea's reliance on its senior players threw the team's campaign in Germany into disarray.

'The players who should normally be our star players, like Park Ji-sung at Manchester United and Seol Ki-hyeon at Reading, [the uncontracted] Ang Jung-hwan, all came to the national team injured or not having played for months at their club teams,' he told me. 'So instead of coming to us as the big-name players and the players who take the lead in the team, they had to struggle just to get into shape in those four weeks. I have to be honest, they didn't do that. They didn't do what we expected them to do.

'Now we have some very interesting, young, talented players who played in the World Cup without any experience. They now have that experience, they know what it means to play national team football and they're all very excited about going to the Asian Cup.'

Arnold, however, remained undeterred about what he needed to do in Asia.

'At this moment [my priority] is to introduce players for 2010, but the short-term goal is to win the Asian Cup because if you win it or do well, next time around it makes the qualifying process [for the World Cup] so much easier,' he said. 'Then you can introduce more young players. If I was in the job till 2010, and my goal was solely 2010, then maybe three or four of the older blokes would probably be pushed aside right now. But that's not my job.

'I also believe, and I've looked at other sports, that when you're in a transition period you can't go too quickly—if you can do it gradually and get rid of older players and introduce younger players, over a period of time you're more likely to have success without ruining the confidence of people and the structure of everything.'

Arnold might get his wish and win the Asian Cup with the nucleus of the side that performed with such distinction at Germany 2006, but that doesn't leave a lot of time for putting together the right team for qualifying for the next World Cup. Up to six senior Socceroos—Chipperfield, Aloisi, Viduka, Skoko, Moore, even Schwarzer—could retire or be pushed out after July 2007, which would create a vacuum within the side in the manner of the Chappell/Lillee/Marsh retirements that rocked Australian cricket in the early 1980s. Arnold has recognised the problem and moved to establish a mentoring group within the team to help young players when they come into camp, but his main goal is still to win the Asian Cup and promote his candidacy for beyond. If that means using the personnel that reached the second round in Germany, his attitude is 'So be it'.

It's hard to blame Arnold for adopting this stance. It's the FFA that, in its failure to find a permanent coach and its lacklustre support of its interim solution, will be culpable if Australians find themselves supporting a team of overripe veterans and too-green juniors in the lead-up to South Africa 2010. Ideally, a more even balance needs to be struck, but according to Arnold there's just too much pressure on him to win.

'The demands are of being successful at the Asian Cup. I've expressed my view [to the FFA board of directors]. Why do we have to win our first Asian Cup? We have too much to learn about Asia, we have too much to learn about Asian players, about Asian countries. It's a learning process for us. What I learned from the Kuwait game in Kuwait was enormous. It took a failure for us to learn what we learned.'

Coaching, of course, is not a profession with a single right way of performing. But equally coaches need to adapt their players to their circumstances to assure victory, and when the opportunity was there to kill off Ghana, the Socceroos—their efforts complicated by the heroics of Black Stars goalkeeper Richard Kingston and some straight-out inefficacy in front—didn't take it.

The *Sydney Morning Herald*'s football writer Michael Cockerill, however, was convinced he'd seen the future.

'What [Frank] Lowy has to do—what he simply must do—is issue a public statement so the "interim" can be removed from Arnold's job description,' he wrote the next day. 'Then Lowy's words will have true meaning. The coaching saga has officially become the most boring story of the year.'

A curious statement, considering Cockerill was the one who'd been pushing it without break.

'Arnold has hung in there and has now earned the right to demand an answer from his boss. The case for Arnold to remain in charge until after next year's Asian Cup finals is irrefutable. Six games, three wins, two draws, and a single loss in the heat of Kuwait City. Qualification for the Asian Cup achieved with time to spare, and without having most of his better players available. It's a record, dare we say it, that Guus Hiddink would have been proud of ... the presence of an injured Mark Viduka on the bench yesterday was a clear show of support.'

Balderdash. The 'higher level' Hiddink demanded as a requirement for Australian football in Honiara was not meant to be something that was brought down from the attic and dusted off just when World Cups came around. As Foster described it, 'the players and support staff were happy to see the arse end of Hiddink', but at least the European master had given the Socceroos belief, direction and ambition. Under the more open and approachable Arnold, it seemed the national men's team was back in a holding pattern—a hunch confirmed when the Socceroos returned to London in February 2007 to play a friendly against Denmark.

As expected, the squad announced for the clash was largely the one that Hiddink took to the World Cup and Arnold put out against Ghana and would, barring unforeseen calamities, take to Thailand for the opening rounds of the Asian Cup. Again it was the safe option, one designed to get Arnold across the line, not get the right mix for the national team for the years ahead. These players could perform to the system drummed into them in Germany without the need for Arnold to train up new additions to the side. But when the casualty list lengthened in the days before the match, with a veritable batting order of big names ruled out through injury or personal commitments—Schwarzer, Moore, Neill, Culina, Bresciano, Beauchamp, Wilkshire, Viduka—Arnold was forced to improvise, and the performance that followed reflected this gun-barrel planning.

The new centre-back pairing of Patrick Kisnorbo and Michael Thwaite was bamboozled, the two inexperienced Socceroos frequently opting to hoof the ball downfield rather than patiently build attacks out from the back. Allowed too much latitude by Grella dropping back deep to help the defenders and by Emerton and Chipperfield playing a more unconstricted role than Hiddink would have allowed them, the Danish forwards Jon Dahl Tomasson and Dennis Rommedahl cut Australia to pieces with low, fast, one-touch passing. They established almost total control of the midfield. As Hiddink had intuited, Josip Skoko was slow chasing down lost possession and Aloisi, playing Viduka's customary role as a lone, ball-holding striker, was frequently called offside and had few runners working off him. In attack, the pickings were slim: midfielder Brett Holman demonstrated some facility for creating chances for his forwards and Sterjovski showed glimpses of his form against Croatia, but that was it. In the 37th minute, when Tomasson hammered the Danes' third goal into goalkeeper Michael Petkovic's sagging net, Arnold, staring blankly from the sideline, looked as though he'd aged 20 years. The game ended 3-1 to the Danes.

This wasn't what Australia's coach had wanted so soon after the encouraging showing against Ghana, especially just months out from the Asian Cup. The usual excuses were advanced—missing players, inadequate preparation, hitting the woodwork—but it had been an undeniably retrograde performance. Danish coach Morten Olsen's post-match comment that the Australians were 'a very physical team' was a blast from the past Arnold could have done without. More worrying, though, is that it was the sort of performance that will become more common unless some tough decisions are made.

In theory it's far better for a team of young players to lose and learn in an Asian Cup than when it matters most—in World Cup qualifying campaigns or World Cups. And as any coach will tell you, the problem with maintaining a 'higher level' of play is that at some point they usually slip. So is it happening now under Arnold?

According to the man himself, the succession has been

seamless. Technical and tactical levels have been maintained, the team spirit is just as strong as it was in Germany, and the players are fully behind him. So, then, what of the view expressed by Viduka, Kewell, Schwarzer and others that we need a European coach?

'The only thing I'll say there is they said that before I was in charge,' Arnold said. 'They've only known me as a good cop for five or six years. I'm not boasting, but Hiddink doesn't give accolades very easily. Probably the biggest accolade he could have given me was him coming out and saying I was ready for the job, that [the FFA] should give me the job.

'To be fair to the players, they didn't know that. I think I proved to them—you can see by the effort level and the way they're playing—that I've gone from being the good cop to the bad cop, and I'm prepared to make hard decisions, and tactically on the training field I know what I'm doing. So they feel a lot more relaxed now, because since the Paraguay game no one's said anything anymore. I haven't seen a player come out and say that we need a top European coach now.'

Arnold mustn't have read a piece in the *Sydney Morning Herald* on 27 October, three weeks after the Paraguay game, which contained quotes from Kewell that made headlines around the world.

'I think you need a leader in any team,' said the convalescing Liverpool winger, 'and we need that for the Australian team ... [Hiddink] was one of the best managers I've ever worked for, and I think if we can get someone even half as good as him, we'll go a long way.'

If Kewell, never the most erudite of players, was trying to imply that Arnold, though 'doing a great job', was not even half as good as Hiddink, he made a fine fist of it.

Craig Foster, one of Arnold's most persistent and vocal critics, believes that Arnold should never have been offered the job. It takes some courage to air this opinion publicly, especially when

Arnold is a former team-mate, but it's a conclusion Foster came to when he looked at the system in place in France, a veritable factory for world-class coaches.

'My concern with Arnold is his level of ability and experience,' Foster told me. 'In order to coach in France, even at the Ligue 1 level, candidates have to do a four-year degree and in the last year they have to go overseas for six months to a club in Italy or Holland or whatever, and when they come back they have to do a thesis, which they then have to present to 500 coaches in a seminar at Clairefontaine [the Fernand Sastre National Technical Centre, regarded as the finest football academy in the world]. Then they have to start at a particular level, then they go to Ligue 1, then they become national coach. Arnold has been in a wonderfully privileged position to learn off Hiddink. But his next step is to take charge either of one of the junior national teams or, at best, the Olyroos. Your first senior coaching role in my view shouldn't be with the senior national team. I think that's ridiculous.'

When I put Foster's comments to Arnold, he wouldn't have a bar of it.

'I'm halfway through my UEFA A-licence, I'm doing all the other badges, I have the highest accreditation I can get here in Australia,' he said. 'Nearly every A-League coach doesn't have that. I had 90 games as a player [for Australia]. I played six years in Europe. I didn't play with a blindfold on. And I've been assistant or been in the coaching staff for at least a hundred games, been to an Olympics and two Confederations Cups. How much experience do you have to have?'

What about a club in Europe? After all, the former Socceroos striker had been offered a job at Roda, which he passed up to take over from Hiddink.

'The coaching licence is the problem,' retorted Arnold. 'It's not easy. How many Australian coaches have gone to Europe?'

'Er, none.'

'Because we're back to like the mid-'80s as footballers where when I first went away, the attitude was, "You play soccer in Australia?" They had no idea. It's the same on the coaching level. We've got to prove ourselves as coaches.'

Precisely. This is where I feel there is a conceit that both Arnold and his employers, the FFA, have failed to recognise. As a football nation we expect our senior-team players to ideally come from the highest tier clubs in Europe—and, with a few exceptions, they do. Kewell is on the books with Liverpool, Culina plays for PSV Eindhoven, Bresciano for Palermo. It shows how far we have come in just a few short decades to be able to expect such standards of our personnel. But our coach? He can't get a job in Europe because he hasn't earned his licence. Arnold's appointment, from any which way you care to view it, is decidedly not of the highest tier. To borrow his own analogy, as a coach he's a throwback to the 1980s.

Familiarity with his players is something no one could begrudge Arnold. But familiarity is not enough to make a world-class coach. Nor is enthusiasm. We saw how both qualities weren't enough to save Farina—and they won't save Arnold beyond the Asian Cup, a situation, to his credit, he readily acknowledges.

In the meantime, the FFA's head of high performance, John Boultbee, is impressed with the way Australia's interim coach is handling the pressure.

'Graham's doing a great job. He's growing,' he said. 'The pleasing thing is with Guus we developed a character in the team that is continuing—as best illustrated in the Ghana match—and that's great. It's a tribute to Graham and the players. And his communication is good; it's good working with him and I think he's doing a great job. I don't think he's feeling unduly pressured.'

The man who calls all the shots, Frank Lowy, is similarly unfussed.

'He's doing quite well,' he said. 'I think Arnold needs another top-line coach with him and then he'll probably be better than what he is now. He has learned a lot under Hiddink and he may learn again under the next one.'

The FFA and its minions have certainly cast their net wide in search of the right man to replace Arnold, with all kinds of names being thrown into the mix—Leo Beenhakker, Carlos Bilardo, Hans Ooft, Jose Pekerman, Sven-Göran Eriksson, Jürgen Klinsmann, Louis van Gaal and Gérard Houllier. Many different coaches from different footballing cultures, which suggests the governing body of Australian football is not making the mistake of trying to find a Hiddink doppelgänger, as South Korea did with Jo Bonfrere and Dick Advocaat.

It's becoming increasingly obvious that Hiddink, for the short time we had him, was one of a kind. Just as it's increasingly obvious that an Australian battler who once played in Holland does not a Dutch supercoach make.

CHAPTER TEN · THE GOOD DIE YOUNG

'Australian football still has a long way to go. We've got a generation much like Croatia had eight years ago—after that generation disappeared, they really struggled. A lot of work needs to be done.'

STEVE HORVAT,
FORMER SOCCEROOS DEFENDER, 2006

Off the Hume Highway at Warwick Farm, outside the front of Peter Warren Ford—a car lot so big it might as well be a suburb in itself—stands an enormous replica of the Sydney Harbour Bridge. It's probably more familiar to residents of the city's sprawling southwestern suburbs than the real thing 40 kilometres away. Harry Kewell, Mark Bosnich, Mark Schwarzer, Paul Okon, Jason Culina, Nick Carle and many other top-flight footballers all grew up and played their formative seasons out here, the greatest nursery of talent anywhere in the country.

It's also where Rale Rasic is building a football academy on 34 acres, opposite the infamous Orange Grove factory outlet, the supposedly illegal development that was forced to close down in 2004. Rasic's partner, Croatian-Australian businessman Edmond Parilo, has visions of the land being a kind of footballing utopia for those who are willing to pay good money for their kids to be trained here by Rasic and his collection of ex-Socceroo assistants, many of whom are currently out of work. The ambitions are as crystallised as they are lofty: to get six- to 18-year-olds from all over the world—but especially Asia—coming here to train 48 weeks a year on its 15 dedicated football pitches. Special netted areas, special heading devices, the works.

Gough Whitlam has done the sod-turning ceremony. The Wikipedia entry has been typed up. The concrete has been poured for the changing rooms. As a tracksuited Rasic elaborated as he escorted me around the rolling grounds, there'll be facilities for disabled kids, mothers who need to change their babies' nappies, everything.

'I want to create *Hollywood?* he beamed, clasping my wrist. Our 1974 World Cup coach likes to hold on to people when he talks. It can be unnerving.

With its electronic gates and patrolling German shepherds, the compound is more like the New Jersey suburbia of Tony Soprano than Tinseltown. When we returned to the main building, Parilo, a large and evidently wealthy man, was about to head off to have dinner with the then-NSW opposition leader, Peter Debnam. He was sweating profusely inside his new suit, his secretary trailing behind him as he stepped into a chauffeured car.

Parilo wasn't giving away his land to Rasic because of altruism. Despite fading memories of the 1974 Socceroos, there's still money to be made from the name Rale Rasic. Importantly, Parilo also owns the rights to put up billboard advertising along the perimeter of his land holding—a licence to print money. He hadn't wasted any time. Already, at the junction of the highway and the entrance to Orange Grove there was a huge likeness of Rasic spruiking the new development.

But why had Rasic got involved? He's 70, the charcoal hair has turned to Leslie Nielsen white, he has grandkids. Why does he need the stress? When the academy was opened by Whitlam, no FFA representative made the trip out to Liverpool. He certainly wasn't getting any favours from the big boys in College Street. But undeniably the man has an ego. He relishes playing the part of Former World Cup Coach™ and most assuredly is not trying to hide from anyone. 'SOCCEROO74' is the number plate on his Mercedes.

'Youth teams is Australia's biggest problem,' he told me. 'Ever since 1999 we have gone to sleep. We are going into year eight since then. No one is answerable. Who's going to replace the Harry Kewells, the Mark Vidukas?'

As anyone who has ever met him will attest, Rasic has an opinion on everything, and sometimes his opinions can last for a very long time. At moments, it's hard to get him to stop talking. Pick a topic, any topic. Ange Postecoglou: 'Lives under 500 lucky stars in this world to keep that position for so long.' Coaching appointments at the National Training Centres (NTCs): 'Extra *ordinary* appointments.' On Ron Smith getting a job with Perth Glory in the A-League: 'How that miracle happens?' On Graham Arnold and John Kosmina forming a successful partnership: 'I become Pol Pot.'

As opinionated as he is, Rasic is still a man without a job. It has obviously pained him that he can't get anyone at the FFA to reply to his letters, that he has to deal with a head of high performance who has never kicked a football. In the FFA's eyes, he is yesterday's man. There is some truth to this. But Rasic thinks he knows better, and starting the Rale Rasic International Football Academy is his way of telling the FFA he isn't about to go away anytime soon. It's hard not to admire what he is trying to do despite some very big obstacles. Why? Because he's absolutely right.

As Australian fans have discovered since the World Cup, the lack of depth in the sport once you remove the senior Socceroos from the equation is an enduring problem. Indeed, our recent record in youth football is dire—the under-17s failed to qualify for the Asian Cup and the under-20s failed to qualify for the World Cup. Our young footballers have one of the best national sports institutes in the world at which to train, the FFA receives more than its fair share of government funding, and the sport has the highest junior participation rate of any code in the country. All things considered, the generous input and the barren output is a veritable scandal.

Rasic's friend and former assistant, Les Scheinflug, who led the Joeys to the final of the FIFA Under-17 World Cup in New Zealand in 1999 and, like Rasic, is cooling his heels in enforced semi-retirement, held a similarly gloomy outlook on Australia's future stocks. In truth, he was hopping mad.

'[The FFA] have done nothing,' he said. 'You have a look at how many junior players have come through into the national senior men's team since I left. We have gone backwards. We have done nothing as far as coaching coaches is concerned, we have done very little in the institutes of sport. If the head of the fish smells and they're not doing their job—I'm talking about [FFA] head office—if they're saving money on preparation, then I will criticise them.'

Scheinflug wasn't short of ammunition. After the under-17s' embarrassing scoreless draw against Laos—hardly a football superpower—in February 2006, men's youth coach Postecoglou had hoped to restore his reputation at the AFC Youth Championship in India in November that year. If he guided the Young Socceroos to the semis, qualification for the 2007 Under-20 FIFA World Cup in Canada was assured.

Instead, China beat the juniors 1-0 in their opening game, meaning Australia finished second in their group. The hiccup was costly: a date with South Korea in the quarter-finals. And so a team containing David Williams, Kaz Patafta, Dario Vidosic, Nathan Burns, Bruce Djite and Matthew Spiranovic—some of the best young players in Australia—came up short, losing to the Koreans 2-1 and missing out on the all-important semis.

According to Scheinflug, preparation and discipline is the key to success. Postecoglou's teams, he argued, had neither. The FFA was squarely to blame.

'They did nothing in Laos. They had a couple of training sessions and went across there a few days before the match. It was worse than what happened with [Tiko Jelisavcic] in Cairns in 1965.

'Now I class myself as a very experienced coach. I have

always been criticised for being a strict disciplinarian but when you look at things now—Craig Moore [being stood down in Sydney], players being sent home from Tahiti [by Frank Farina], the Frank Arok days when people used fire extinguishers in the hotel and did other things—then you say Les Scheinflug was right-on, spot-on.

'Before the World Cup, Brett Emerton's father Mick came to see me, and said to me, "Hey, Les, Brett says thanks for being so strict because he would never have made it if you didn't teach him." These are things that I think are important. We can pinch a bit from the Europeans and South Americans as far as discipline off the park is concerned.'

Youth development isn't the sexiest subject that Australia's new football administrators need to come to grips with, but it is the most pressing issue facing the game for the next 20 to 30 years. For all the success of the Socceroos in Germany and their ambitions at the Asian Cup, no house that was ever built from the top down can expect to stay standing.

Since the election of Frank Lowy as FFA chairman in 2003, everyone from former players to soccer mums and dads in suburban parks had been warning about the dangers of ignoring the youth issue. While World Cup qualification was great, and the A-League was as good as could be expected just two seasons in, those achievements disguised the unsettling reality that Australia's youth teams were dead ducks. No youth league was affiliated with the existing eight A-League franchises. The training offered to kids in NTCs and institutes was inferior to the best instruction offered in Europe. There was no incentive for A-League coaches to pick green young players over wizened veterans. Unfortunately for the FFA, these deep-seated cultural and structural issues boiled over when the Young Socceroos went to India.

Craig Foster, who in the weeks afterwards got involved in a heated on-air stoush with Postecoglou, had seen the writing on the wall for a long time.

'Youth development is where my great passion is. I continually bang on on SBS about it, and it's a lonely role to be honest,' he said. 'The result in Laos was probably the worst ever. Results in football happen, but performances just don't happen. [At the 2005 Under-17 FIFA World Cup] in Peru, Australia played in a strong group. We had Mexico and Turkey, who both made the top four—Mexico won it—and Uruguay. But the style of our football was "old football".

'No one's teaching our kids to keep possession. No one's teaching our kids to do a tactical build-up. We're spending millions of dollars in these NTCs around the country and I can see the results every time our youth teams play. If it was me, I'd sack the lot of them tomorrow. It's a waste of taxpayers' money.

'In 2005 John Boultbee reappointed the four-year contracts of directors of the NTCs, one of the worst things this whole regime has done. The NTCs have set us back decades. We used to produce better players when they were produced in Sydney Croatia, Marconi, Sydney Olympic, because they were produced under a cultural style. Viduka didn't play rubbish football for Melbourne Knights juniors. They wanted him to play like [Croatia legend Zvonimir] Boban. The key years are 13 to 15. In France, the best young kids are put into Clairefontaine. In Australia, we throw them in with coaches who aren't worth two cents.'

Boultbee, a former director of the AIS and self-admitted football neophyte, shrugged off the criticism.

'It's ignorant and it's ill-informed, and it's typical,' he said. 'It's not recognising the qualities of the people in the institutes. There are good people in the institutes, there are some that need changing, there are some that have been changed, which Craig chooses not to recognise. We made changes at the national level, too, which he chooses not to recognise ... he probably doesn't even know the names of the coaches.

'[The FFA would] really welcome something constructive coming out of Craig. It's not fair to subject people to the ill-informed badgering that you get on SBS and maybe that doesn't help the FFA but nobody deserves what some people have had to put up with there. [Foster's interview with Postecoglou was] not an attempt to have an informed discussion; on the contrary, it was pushing a barrow for the sake of pushing a barrow. It was a disgrace. It was journalism at its lowest level.'

A bizarre statement—especially since SBS has historically done more for the game in this country than any other network—but ultimately more sad than wacky. Though Frank Lowy assured me he had a 'very good relationship with Les Murray' and said he wasn't sure 'whether there is any strain' between the national broadcaster and the FFA, the truth is that relations between the two are at an all-time low. The rot began with Farina's and now Arnold's refusal to appear on the network (though Arnold insisted he'd never been invited, a claim one SBS insider said was not true), carried over in John O'Neill's attempts to silence criticism of the FFA when a new TV deal was being brokered in 2005, and probably hit rock-bottom with the Foster-Postecoglou contretemps.

Boultbee and his colleagues must bear some responsibility for the breakdown. In the FFA's ideal world, every football commentator would be Lee Furlong and every football journalist would be a 19-year-old AAP cadet. But it doesn't work that way in football. Football people are passionate. Success doesn't mean that criticism simply has to stop. Criticism can be as constructive as it is confrontational.

Yet SBS is not without blame either. The network has long regarded itself as judge and jury on all matters football, and when it lost its TV rights to Fox Sports, some parties within and outside the network believed its editorial judgment became compromised by bitterness.

Foster has never been popular at the FFA—he's forthright and fearless in his stance—but he made himself Public Enemy Number One in late 2005 when Federation Française de Football (FFF) technical director and World Cup-winning coach

Aimé Jacquet came to Australia without the official blessing of the authorities. (The FFF is regarded as one of the benchmarks for youth development anywhere in the world.) It had been an initiative hatched by Foster while he was chief executive of players' body the Australian Professional Footballers' Association (PFA). According to Foster, when the PFA invited the FFA to endorse the seminar, they refused point blank. O'Neill, he claimed, was spitting chips.

'[The fact that] O'Neill was threatened, even went so far as to say he felt pressured, was just incredible,' said Foster. 'For a football country that has never opened our eyes to what the rest of the world offers—has just begun that through Hiddink but hasn't gone beyond that because his knowledge hasn't gone outside the Socceroos—for a culture in which that had been our main problem, for someone like the chief executive to be so negative, I found it amazing. The argument's almost like: "Unless we educate you, you've got no right to education."

'Jacquet came and gave an honest assessment of Australian players and everyone was up in arms: "Oh, how can he say that?" Well, because it's the truth. Hiddink said the same thing. He came in and said: "I played against you in 2001 in the Confederations Cup with South Korea, and I assessed Australia and I found them to be very open, tactically very easy to beat."

'The real beauty of it is this: if we couldn't achieve a more technical, tactical game, if we are just physical thugs, then fair enough. But Hiddink showed what we are capable of. What can he do and what can we do in ten years of proper instruction for our kids? We need a national debate on the way we want to play football. People want to identify a style. And we need to have a picture of the way we want to play and I think it's important for the kids.'

At least now, with Jacquet back at Clairefontaine and the ambitions of the Joeys and Young Socceroos in a thousand little pieces, the FFA has belatedly recognised the predicament Australian football is in.

In late 2006, three important developments took place that suggest football's national body is getting serious about planning for the future. The first was the decision of the FFA and Football Federation Victoria to accept an AIS team into the Victorian Premier League. Now, instead of playing *Pro Evolution Soccer 6* in their bedrooms, Australia's most promising football students can play week in, week out, in the country's best state competition.

The second development was the dispatching of former players Andy Harper and Alistair Edwards on separate missions to Japan, the United States, South America and Europe to review youth development practices abroad as part of a Talent Identification and Development Review. ('Our aim was not to tinker around the edges,' Harper told me. 'Qualifying for the World Cup was big and setting up the A-League from nothing was big, but modelling the future of the game is a massive job.')

The final initiative, however, was probably the most far-reaching. The announcement in early December that Dutchman Robert Baan would take up the FFA's talismanic position of technical director in June 2007 came totally out of left field. Though his name had little of the traction of other candidates who'd been mooted for the job, careful scrutiny of Baan's career suggested the FFA had recruited wisely. Senior coaching experience in the Eredivisie and with the Dutch national team, a long-time interest and immersion in youth football, and solid experience setting up development programs in the Middle East were precisely the sort of career building blocks that someone charged with repaving Australia's football pathways needed to possess to gain instant respect. More importantly, Baan's brief was to immediately deal with Australia's faltering men's youth teams, spiking Postecoglou from his twin responsibilities and appointing separate coaches. He would also step in and assume responsibility for the under-23s from Arnold. After years of inertia, it was almost too much to process.

Youth teams, coaching licences, what style of football our national teams should adopt—it's a sign of how far the local game has progressed under Lowy that these issues, so long ignored by various administrations in their mad quests to qualify for the World Cup, are now being spoken about openly. That there is lively debate is even better.

The endgame for everyone within the football community, whether they are inside the FFA or pushed to the margins, is to see Australian football prosper for decades to come. Nobody, not even the most fairweather football fan, wants to see Australia's performance at Germany 2006 go down in history as a freak accident. It made us all feel good. It *meant* something. Who wouldn't want it to happen again?

The FFA has played out of its skin in recruiting Hiddink, qualifying for the World Cup, consolidating the A-League, bringing in Baan. Fair play to them. But just as quickly as those achievements came about, they can also be taken away. It's how the FFA handles a lot of the 'second-tier' issues that will ultimately determine how history will judge its *contribution* to Australian football. And that is an important distinction to make. The FFA is not of itself Australian football. The game is and will always be bigger than any one organisation or individual—sometimes, sadly, this is forgotten.

As someone who has worked first-hand in the fledgling professional leagues of America and Asia and seen the Socceroos play at the World Cup, South Korea's assistant coach Afshin Ghotbi is a well-placed and refreshingly neutral candidate to make a call on how Australia is progressing as a football nation. What he told me will not please everybody.

For all the growing pains the Australian game has gone through since the recruitment of Hiddink in mid-2005, this credentialled technical analyst still saw an English style in our national team. More surprisingly, Ghotbi believed the Socceroos hadn't shown anything that could fairly be described as 'Dutch flair' in Germany.

'You saw some sequences in Germany where [the Socceroos] tried to build the game out of the back but in most cases it was no more than a few passes and the ball was being played into the box,' Ghotbi said. 'All the chances came from playing direct and looking for second balls and the individual actions of the players in the box. It's a difficult style to play against.

'Australia has some difficult challenges. The domestic league needs to improve a lot to reach the top level in football. The other challenge is that the distances to travel are so far. It makes it very difficult for players to give their best performances. The challenge in Asia is that the domestic leagues are not good enough for the top level. The players who go abroad are megastars. When they come back to the national team they have so many demands placed on them, by agents, sponsors, the media.

'But Australia being added to the AFC is a very good thing. The style, power and the directness of your football offers something a little bit different to most Asian football. It will make Asian football richer.

'I hope the FFA takes the right steps and tries to build a long-term infrastructure to consistently produce good footballers for the Australian national team. It's no accident that certain countries are producing good players and good teams year after year and World Cup after World Cup. It all starts with talent—how that talent is developed from young ages through to the professional leagues. Then it goes with the federation's vision with the youth national teams and the senior national team. And putting coaches with experience and motivation in to really build football for the long term.'

He could have taken the words right out of my mouth.

CHAPTER ELEVEN · OLD SOCCER BLUES

'He who does not know where he comes from does not know where he is going.'

RALE RASIC, 2006

Still basking in the afterglow of the world cup, John O'Neill addressed the National Press Club in Canberra in late July 2006. He told an eager audience of journalists, businesspeople and bureaucrats that football was 'almost unrecognisable from the morass of old soccer's administration', and that the key plank of his and Frank Lowy's work at the FFA, the A-League, was 'new football's shopfront'.

O'Neill could be forgiven for his hubris. What was there to complain about? A second-round berth at Germany, money in the bank, a strongly supported domestic competition, a huge deal with Fox Sports, a director on the board using his influence to push the game in the Fairfax press, a vice-president in FIFA, a new home in Asia—the ticks on the shopping list ran off the page.

So it defied reason that a man who was enjoying the peak of his career as a sports administrator—winning a Rugby World Cup included—would decide to walk away from the game altogether a month later. Especially so when he had come into the job declaring that he 'would not want to leave unfinished business' and was planning to stay on for 'at least five years'. But at a press conference at 5 pm on 29 August, Lowy explained his chief executive's decision not to renew his contract as a need 'for a change of direction'. O'Neill said he'd suffered under an 'incredibly intensive and demanding workload' and that after over a decade pumping hands for the ARU and FFA he'd 'like to think about what is possible in other fields of endeavour'. Most observers surmised that the real reason for O'Neill's departure was the pair's tense working relationship, something O'Neill had euphemistically described in one interview as 'creative tension ... sure, we butt heads'. Both men had reputations for being headstrong, demanding, egotistical. That they'd managed to stay together so long was probably the biggest shock of all.

There were other theories. One was the fallout from their reputedly heated clash over the future of Frank Farina after the 2005 Confederations Cup. Lowy wanted Farina out, but O'Neill was said to have refused to cut him adrift. After all, he'd personally guaranteed Farina's position, confirming publicly early that year that the Australia coach had a contract that went through to the end of the qualifying campaign and would be honoured no matter what. That clearly didn't happen. If one widely held rumour is to be believed, O'Neill threatened to quit if Farina was sacked. Lowy denied this when I put it to him.

'There was no such issue [of quitting] on the table,' he said. 'It was a consensus among us that we needed to replace Frank Farina.'

Another theory, this one emanating from the corridors of the Australian Sports Commission in Canberra, is that after the World Cup, where he'd been dazzled by the klieg lights of FIFA, O'Neill had indicated to Lowy his desire to move on from his post as chief executive and enter the FIFA gravysphere in a more senior role. He'd admitted previously that he found 'the FIFA and Asian federation side of it ... really fascinating, it's such a big game, it dwarfs anything else I've ever been involved in'. But when I asked Lowy if O'Neill had ever expressed to him a desire to move on to FIFA, he said he had no knowledge of the subject.

Whatever the story, O'Neill's legacy for Australian football was a mixed bag. World Cup qualification, the establishment of the A-League and Australia's entry into Asia were all substantial achievements, but they were the work of many hands, not least Lowy's. These 'big-ticket' issues all required a man of Lowy's vision, wealth and international clout to get over the line.

What is perhaps more telling when speaking of O'Neill's contribution is to look at what he didn't do. He didn't stay on to see the Socceroos play at the 2007 Asian Cup, probably a more profound achievement in a sociological, political and historical context than qualifying for the World Cup. He didn't stick around to appoint Robert Baan. He didn't oversee an effective World Cup ticketing process—it was shambolic. And by the end of 2006, Soccer NSW, Australia's largest football association, still hadn't implemented the recommendations of the Crawford Report, the government-backed inquiry into Australian football that had ushered in the Lowy era.

Then there was O'Neill's confrontational style of diplomacy. His combative stance early in his tenure on the club-versus-country issue disenchanted Harry Kewell, Mark Viduka and other senior Socceroos. His public comments about stepping in to host the 2010 World Cup should South Africa fail to meet its construction deadlines caused a political headache—FIFA and the FFA's media department had to intercede to avert an international incident.

Yet O'Neill left his successor, Ben Buckley, a former suit with the AFL, in a very privileged position from which to bed down all the game's gains. The youth issue has been examined and the right man appointed to implement a coherent vision for the game. The stubborn redoubt of Soccer NSW remains, but it cannot live in perpetuity as an island.

Buckley's candidacy is all the more visionary as he comes from a sport that has had to look *within* for its survival. AFL's inherent flaw—its immobility—has created a need to nurture the grassroots. For too long football has treated its own grassroots with contempt. The fact that an old Soccer Australia levy slapped on registered junior players is still in existence, despite the federal government's millions, the windfall from the World Cup, the Fox contract and a whopping new Nike sponsorship deal, is indicative that all is not so neat and tidy behind the gleaming shopfront.

The shelves might be groaning, the aisles might be humming with customers, but all the filled stadiums and marketing claptrap in the world cannot conceal some troubling issues that just won't go away for Australian football. 'Old soccer' ain't done yet.

In his unpretentious, 1960s-era home in the hills near Liverpool, out beside the leaf-covered pool, Rale Rasic spends a lot of his time in his office-cum-den. It has all the accoutrements you would expect in a middle-aged man's bolthole: a desk, a miniature globe, photos on the walls, souvenir mugs, a telephone, a bookshelf piled willy-nilly with well-thumbed paperbacks ranging from fitness manuals to Billy Connolly biographies. The grey afternoon I visited, Rasic bade me inside and sat back in his black leather armchair, inviting me to gaze at the pennants of old combatants and the framed pictures of celebrities and dignitaries who'd entered his orbit during his charmed life: Guus Hiddink, Gough Whitlam, Bob Marley, Cathy Freeman. Our 1974 World Cup coach had seen and done a lot. But I hadn't seen anything yet.

With a flourish, he pulled back a sliding door to reveal a cave of Socceroos treasures: the black boots of 1974 captain Peter Wilson, a jersey signed by the entire team that beat Hong Kong in 1973 to put Australia through to its first World Cup, a watchband made of gold presented to him by the Shah of Iran. But the showpiece was the full handmade uniform of Jim Scane, the Socceroos' human mascot in 1974.

'WIR FÜRCHTEN NIEMAND! MY BLOODY OATH MATE!' it read in sparkling gold on one trouser leg. On the other: 'HURRA WIR SIND DA! FAIR DINKUM MATE!' On the back of the jacket, crossed out in red flock strips, were the names of the countries defeated in the 1973 qualifying campaign—New Zealand, Iraq,

Indonesia, Iran, South Korea—followed by their unmarked and undefeated World Cup opponents. For all its breathtaking gaudiness, the costume had a sort of poignant innocence about it. I told Rasic it belonged in a museum. His face turned red.

'I am still waiting on a reply from a letter I wrote to John O'Neill on 14 May 2003, when he was appointed,' he said, fixing me with a stare. 'I suggested we meet to discuss issues over the establishment of an Australian Football Museum. I wrote that it is a shame and embarrassment that André Krüger in Hanover has the greatest collection of Australian football memorabilia in the world. I wrote to O'Neill on three occasions and never got a reply.'

He wasn't likely to get one anytime soon, either.

Slighted, Rasic was now moving his entire collection to the site of his and Edmond Parilo's academy at Cumberland Grove, where it would be housed in a special building. It seemed especially unfortunate that such a collection was being passed up by the FFA, but like anything that pre-dated the arrival of Lowy, it simply wasn't a priority.

For an alternative history of the past few years in Australian football, all you need to do is speak with a former Socceroo. There, you'll find stories the FFA doesn't want you to know. Like Ted Smith's. The 1956 Olympian is the convener for the Socceroo Club, an infrequent gathering of Socceroos alumni that was founded just before the Iran match in 1997. On that fateful day, at the expense of the old Soccer Australia, the members of the club were flown into Melbourne and treated to a motorcade tribute around the ground. But for the past two years, in attempting to get some official recognition, Smith has had little joy.

For all the faults of the administrations that came before the FFA, and there were many, they at least did the right thing by the veterans of the game. The sport's governing body has agreed in principle to the idea of a Socceroo Club but is protective of the future of its brand. When Smith tried to register 'Socceroo

Club' with the Australian Securities and Investments Commission, he found it was protected. The Socceroo Club charter proposes that former Socceroos 'contribute to the future growth of Australian football and not be lost to the game' and outlines, among many other ambitions, its desire to create a museum of Socceroos memorabilia, an opportunity that, with Rasic now making his own plans, may be forever lost.

Smith's primary objective, though, is to gain some financial support and recognition from the FFA, not for it to be involved in the club's day-to-day affairs. As he explained it to me, many former players want to give something back to the game but—either by design or neglect—are being shut out. When the 2006 Socceroos left for their great adventure in Germany, for example, the 1974 version was not asked to play any part in any official farewells or other functions, which caused, according to John Watkiss, 'a bit of resentment; we were pretty much snubbed by the FFA'. Added Ray Baartz: 'The FFA missed a great opportunity in not bringing in the '74 boys.'

'It's not unfair to say [the FFA] doesn't appreciate former players,' ventured Smith. 'Not one former Socceroo has been nominated to be a life member. They say things like, "Yes, we want to do these things," but it's always a low priority. It's a matter of do you have enough will to make it happen. The FFA could have the greatest PR of all time for nothing.'

John Boultbee told me that there wasn't a lack of willingness to help the Socceroo Club but the FFA simply couldn't action all its plans simultaneously. It came down to time and resources.

'We have been slow,' he conceded. 'But that's simply because we've been preoccupied with other things. It's always been the whole organisation's intention to embrace those who've served the game well, particularly the players. We are now recognising the former Socceroos with caps, and that's been in the melting pot for a long time. It was sort of put on the bottom of the list when we had our World Cup qualification and our new league to organise, and all sorts of other things. It's not been a case of:

"Bugger them." It's been a case of: "Yes, we must, if only we had time to get that one off the ground." And eventually we have.'

Yes, but only up to a point. When the Socceroo Club asked the FFA prior to the Bahrain Asian Cup qualifier in Sydney if it could hand out the baggy green-style numbered caps to its latest honourees on the pitch, they were told they could not. It didn't fit into the program. Smith had to organise his own function room at the Sydney Cricket Ground next door. So while the Qantas choir was boring the crowd stiff with the latest murder of Peter Allen's 'I Still Call Australia Home', some of the true legends of Australian football were next door, stumping up $20 from their own pockets to help pay for a few fizzy drinks, party pies and sausage rolls. Boultbee was there, doling out his caps from a cardboard box.

'It was the worst bloody corporate box you've ever seen in your life,' said Craig Foster, who got his cap that night. 'It was a fucking toilet. There was no lectern, nothing. Inside the hats it bloody said, "CRICKET". They were cricket hats. It's a baggy green but on it it says, "FOOTBALL FEDERATION AUSTRALIA". To his credit, Boultbee at least came and Baartzey handed out the caps. If it hadn't been him handing them out, I would have fucking completely spat it. But I thought I'm getting them from a legend. I spoke to Ted and I said, "What's up with this?" He said, "We asked the FFA if they could hand out the hats before half-time or on the pitch. They wouldn't even come back to us on that." It doesn't surprise me. You've got the history of the game in a different stadium. I mean, it's fucking unbelievable. It wouldn't happen in rugby.'

Baartz was more diplomatic than Foster but no less annoyed by the snub.

'The FFA is certainly taking a step in the right direction by giving out these caps, but I think it would have been nice to get the crowd involved,' he said. 'What we're trying to do with the Socceroo Club is build a bit of tradition in the game. One of the things that has been lacking with football is we've tended to neglect our past and haven't respected the people who have been there and done that as much as we probably should.'

Former Socceroos captain Paul Wade, who was also at the SCG function, concurred: 'There are lots of positives coming along but I totally agree with those people that "formers" have been unbelievably ignored.'

The tempestuous Rasic, meanwhile, refused on principle to attend the gathering. He felt that until the FFA gave full recognition to former Socceroos and actually dug into their own pockets to pay for such events, he would play no part in them. At the same time that Baartz was handing out caps at the SCG, Rasic was fronting up to the ticket window at Aussie Stadium, forced, he claimed, into buying his own ticket. It wasn't the first time. For the Uruguay qualifier in November 2005, he'd only got into the ground as a guest of the global financial services company JP Morgan. This time, when he was informed there were no tickets available, a passer-by donated his seat to the 1974 World Cup coach.

Like many of his comrades, 1965 Socceroo Stan Ackerley was disgusted when he had his old Soccer Australia gold card taken away from him by the FFA, one of many cost-cutting measures introduced when the new regime was installed.

'Someone introduced me to John O'Neill at the Hall of Fame dinner about four years ago, and he was like, "Who the hell are you?" I said, "Pleased to meet you," and O'Neill didn't say another word. I'll never forget it. At least give a little bit of respect. The FFA have wiped us out. We can't even get into a game now. They don't want to know us.'

The deal in place now is that former players are offered one free ticket with the option to buy a ticket for their partner. Before, both tickets were offered free of charge. The difference might not sound like much, but for Ackerley and his comrades, many of whom jeopardised both their livelihoods and their personal safety to play for their country in places such as Cambodia and Vietnam in the 1960s and '70s, the offer is an insult.

Said Archie Blue: 'We're treated like anyone else, and I find that rude.'

The unsavoury truth, though, is that Blue and Ackerley can consider themselves lucky. Some of their former team-mates, like goalkeeper John Roberts, don't get offered tickets, free or otherwise, at all.

One of the forgotten pioneers of Australian football, Roberts was lured to England by Chelsea manager Tommy Docherty after the 1965 World Cup qualifiers in Phnom Penh, but became caught in a war of words between the English club and his local club, APIA-Leichhardt, over the £20,000 transfer fee. Docherty grumbled: 'I should expect to buy the whole national Australian team for that sort of money.'

Roberts went on to play for the Blues, Blackburn, Chesterfield, Bradford City and Southend United, making his debut for Rovers against Manchester United in front of 53,000 people. His game in Cambodia was his first and only A-international for Australia, but not because he wasn't up to scratch. When he informed team management halfway through the tour that he was on his way to Stamford Bridge after the World Cup play-offs, he was permanently blacklisted.

'I was told I'd never play for Australia again,' he said, refusing to name the official who rubbed him out. 'Going overseas was taboo. It was not encouraged at all.'

Australia's first World Cup goalkeeper played more than 300 league and cup games in England, but he has yet to be inducted into the Australian Football Hall of Fame. More damningly, he has never been invited to a football game in Australia, by any administration.

'I couldn't care less,' he said, 'but it hurts in the sense that you think they would invite you.'

Boultbee assured me that the FFA was mindful of the resentment over the lack of privileges for former players, but felt the sport's governing body had to put the public first.

'I can understand their disappointment. But they don't see the other side of it—when taxi drivers and all sorts of people were turning up to games with gold passes. Commercially we want to look after the former Socceroos with a free pass and the opportunity to buy one. I'm not pointing the finger at the former Socceroos in this regard, but there has been a freebies culture in the sport. The former Socceroos were just a small group of those who expected, and were given, free access. We have effectively narrowed that so the paying public can get more access.'

This may be the case, but to abolish a just and good-intentioned scheme on the pretext that a handful of people abused it seems heavy-handed. Especially when it involves the true servants of the game—the players. How many tickets are given away to people in the media, for instance, who only turn up when they don't have something better to do? A prominent Sydney sports newsreader at the Uruguay game in Sydney left the ground with his date even before the penalty shootout was taken. He was bored, of all things. It would have taken a hundred tethered oxen to drag away any football fan, least of all a former Socceroo, from watching the end of that unforgettable match.

Old players can feel sidelined for other reasons, though; the administrators aren't always the bad guys. The sad tale of reclusive Socceroos captain Peter Wilson is not, as some have suggested, merely the result of Sir Arthur George welshing on his promises over match payments after the 1974 World Cup, or of Wilson being stuffed around by his club, APIA-Leichhardt. It was the result of years of persistent downplaying and discrediting of his contribution to the Australian game.

Johnny Warren, understandably, never got over not being selected as captain of the 1974 team, writing in his autobiography, 'I feel I should have been captain so it's something I look back on with a great deal of disappointment and regret,' and that 'watching someone else lead the Socceroos out onto the field was like a knife in my side.' This, despite his appearance in a German TV documentary four months before the World Cup saying that his best football years were over and he was contemplating staying at home. Warren, sitting on some unknown Australian beach, was clutching a cigarette and a beer. Just playing football, he said with chilling portent, was not worth giving up the good things in life.

Still, the question of why Warren was not made captain after returning from a career-threatening injury became almost a cause célèbre for his supporters and, from 1974 until his death in 2004, it would get regular airings in the press. Through this long process of complaint, repetition and obfuscation it almost became an accepted fact among the Australian public that not only was Warren captain of that historic side but also that he was the Socceroos' player of the tournament. The myth grows ever greater. In one recently released book about the 2006 World Cup, the author called Warren, who played one game before being dropped, 'the Socceroos' best player during that famous 1974 campaign', which would surely come as a surprise to a lot of his old team-mates, not least Adrian Alston. The reality, his coach Rasic told me, was that Warren was 'lucky' to go to Germany at all.

'Johnny was never the same after his serious operation in 1971,' he said. 'He was told when he was performing shockingly that he will go to the World Cup as a gift for services to the country, not for his form. The captaincy never goes to the player who's never sure he will play.'

Rasic's choice of captain, of course, was Wilson, the recently arrived immigrant from Middlesbrough who'd rocked up at Illawarra's South Coast United and, as Matthew Hall wrote in *The Away Game*, 'cut an imposing figure ... it wasn't just the silk shirts and the flared trousers that got him noticed either. Playing as a sweeper, Wilson was calm under pressure and despite being a quiet bloke off the pitch was a deft organiser on it.' In his seminal work, *Jack Pollard's Soccer Records*, Sid Grant went so far as to describe him as 'an immaculate gentleman—a man for all occasions ... Wilson often brings sunshine to drab, kick and rush type matches'. When Rasic put the choice of Wilson vs Warren to a team vote, 20 out of the 22 votes cast went to Wilson. Wilson abstained.

It was when he'd retired from the game that Wilson began noticing in newspapers descriptions ascribed to Warren as 'captain of Australia's 1974 World Cup team' or 'Captain Socceroo'. Wilson was shattered. Even more so when it got personal. In the Sydney match program for the Australia-Uruguay clash in 2005, for instance, Les Murray, Warren's great friend and staunchest advocate, wrote that Wilson was a 'dull Englishman'.

When I asked Murray why he'd chosen to describe one of Australian football's true immortals that way, he defended it by saying, 'It wasn't criticism of Wilson as a captain, player or man; it's simply that he was no Johnny Warren as a publicity vehicle for the sport. Wilson was a Yorkshireman who spoke in three syllables and had no emotional attachment to promoting Australian football among the Australian masses.'

Rasic was aghast: 'I wish Les Murray would be given the privilege to meet Peter once in his life. He would change his opinion. He's definitely not what Murray and other journalists have written about him. Interview any Socceroo of that era and they will all tell you how great Peter was, and how great his sense of humour was, and what a great leader he was. On the question of dignity, Peter Wilson was the Himalaya—in his attitude, desire, love of friends and respect for every Socceroo that he played with.'

Even his nemesis, Sir Arthur George, agreed Wilson was a tremendous character: 'Peter wasn't a communicator, but he was bloody popular. He was a bloody nice bloke.'

'Johnny didn't have that,' continued Rasic. 'He was always very serious and a different person. You can't make someone funny. People used to fall on the floor when Peter was cracking jokes, and Johnny wouldn't produce a bloody smile. I've met a lot of people, but Johnny was unique in that regard.'

No one can doubt Warren's missionary-like dedication to promoting Australian football, but to denigrate Wilson's character, as Murray and others have done since the player chose self-imposed exile, is unnecessary.

Why did the laughs run out for Wilson? It's a mystery, something known only to the player and a few of his close confidants. Hopefully, if and when our first World Cup captain is ready to tell his own story, something approaching the truth will emerge. Until then, the history of that era of the Australian game shall remain unsatisfactorily one-sided.

The weight of history can overwhelm football sides—one only has to think of Argentina, Brazil and England to see how achievements and the expectations that follow can place a considerable psychological burden on players, coaches and officials. For those teams, anything short of winning is failure. This is something Australia, having played in only two World Cups and embarking on its inaugural Asian Cup campaign, can count as a blessing. Every time our national team takes to a pitch, it is marking new ground. We can play without cynicism, without pressure. But our status as a late-bloomer in world football also betrays a certain cultural innocence. The manner in which we went out of Germany 2006—to a Fabio Grosso dive—spoke volumes about Australia's true position in the world football firmament and how far we really have to go to win a World Cup.

One afternoon just before the Bahrain match in Sydney, I attended a lunchtime lecture by Les Murray at the Lowy Institute for International Policy, a sandstone pile in the middle of Sydney's CBD that the FFA boss had bought and refurbished in 2003. Murray's speech was entitled 'The World Cup: Australia's Success in Football Diplomacy' and in it he propounded fairly well-worn ideas about the popularity of football—globalism, the sport's innate democratic qualities, the tribalism of fans, their loyalty to country—and spoke of the tournament as an 'intercultural feast', all of which was hard to disagree with.

When Murray said he thought the Socceroos could make it to the semi-finals in 2014, I couldn't help but feel he was being too optimistic. How was this possible when the great teams of Europe were prepared to dive to win games and FIFA wasn't doing anything constructive to stop it? Diving historically hadn't been in the Australian football make-up. Didn't this demonstrate a naivete in our football that would keep us exactly where the world wanted us? I stood up and put it to Murray.

'I don't think Australians would support an Australian team that took dives,' he replied. 'I don't believe you have to dive to win the World Cup.'

I still wasn't convinced. But it must have got Murray thinking, because days later he fashioned an editorial, 'Socceroos: Honour for Sale', on *The World Game* website, where he paraphrased my question.

'The Socceroos battled and competed, naively some might say, in a mind devoid of the chicanery that fuels modern modes of football achievement at the elite level ... one didn't see much of this from Brazil, or from the Africans, the Asians nor the Australians. Perhaps it was some kind of naivete. Well if that is what it takes to win a World Cup then I don't want Australia to ever win it and I would rather they stayed naive.'

I couldn't have agreed more with Murray's sentiment—like any football fan I detested diving—but it was the height of naivete of Murray to think the Brazilians and the Africans hadn't thrown themselves around at the World Cup like Lady Macbeth on the castle floor at Inverness. The Brazilians were no lilywhites and the Ghanaians and Ivorians were as bad as the chronically afflicted Portuguese and Italians. The Australians, too, are becoming quite good at milking a penalty. Tim Cahill, Archie Thompson and Harry Kewell have repeatedly been accused of diving during their careers and even Lucas Neill, the hapless victim of Grosso's dying-swan routine, admitted that he would have done the same if he'd been in Grosso's position.

Kewell later echoed that sentiment in a TV interview.

When I spoke to Murray afterwards, he was shocked to hear it. 'I'm disappointed,' he said. 'I've never seen an Australian dive. Some players might have an ideology because they play in the cutthroat world of European football that winning by any means is the most important thing, but it's not part of the Australian culture.'

He's right. It's not—or at least it wasn't until recently. But that's how Australian football, for better or worse, is changing. The Aussie sense of a 'fair go' is incompatible with the world's idea of 'fair play'. FIFA has shown an unwillingness to do anything about diving and simulation—from introducing video replays to enforced temporary removal of 'injured' players off the pitch. So, whether you support diving or not, it's unreasonable to expect our players to stand by gormlessly while some of the best players on the planet—Cristiano Ronaldo, Arjen Robben, Didier Drogba, Adriano—audition for the Russian Ballet and their indecent offences go unpunished. Australia would be an even lonelier place in the atlas of the world game if we were the only country not doing it.

In the Ghana match in London, the Socceroos' only goal came when John Aloisi threw himself in the air after being challenged clumsily from behind by Francis Dickoh, despite video replays showing there had been no contact. Aloisi stepped up and, like he had done in Sydney a year before, coolly converted the penalty. Australia had turned an unexpected and not entirely welcome corner. But we were getting wiser.

Old soccer, new football. To some, such as Frank Lowy, the labels are meaningless; it's just a question of semantics. 'I don't think it should be taken seriously,' he laughed. 'Just because it's old doesn't mean it's bad. It's just old.' To others, such as the 1974 team's Manfred Schaefer, the rewriting of history cuts deep: 'One thing I detested very early on was the FFA had no regard [for the past]. The people that came in were strangers. They had no feeling for football whatsoever. No passion. They didn't want any tradition. The game didn't start when these guys came in.'

Whatever tag applies, football is still played with a ball and two teams of 11. What has changed is Australia. When the Socceroos emerged on the world scene in the 1960s and '70s, the number of foreigners allowed to play in Europe was capped, the local league was semi-professional, there was next to no TV coverage, and sports medicine was a can of magic spray. Mediocrity—and acceptance of that mediocrity—guaranteed tenure for coaches. Nil-all draws were 'triumphs'. With its knockabout heroes such as Johnny Warren and Peter Wilson and its funky tracksuit fashions, it's easy to look back on that era of Australian football with misty-eyed nostalgia, and some within the game have never got over it, clinging to whatever tenuous relevance they still have in a sport that achieves new milestones every day.

The marginalisation back then of what at one time was a robust and well-supported game was a reflection of the social alchemy of the day, when communities of newly arrived immigrants from continental Europe looked out for each other and kept the memories of their homelands alive through their social and football clubs. The Ten Pound Poms didn't need that same outlet because of their common language and shared cultural identity with white Australians.

It was when the children of those immigrants grew up as Australians with their own families that the game should have changed and become mainstream, yet for various political reasons it didn't—and it paid the price. But it wasn't for lack of trying. When the big end of town got the opportunity to take over the game—as it had with Aussie Rules, league, rugby and cricket—all Australians, whatever their background, finally appreciated what had been under their noses all along.

'Anybody who suggests it's all been done in the past couple of years, they're naive. Let's be clear,' mused Basil Scarsella. 'The players that are playing in the current national league came through the junior ranks of Australian football. The World Cup side that did brilliantly in Germany, they didn't come through in the past two years, they came through in the last ten years or more. Let's not ignore the contribution of Sir Arthur George, John Constantine and David Hill. I think in some ways the appointment of Terry Venables set the pattern for the appointment of Guus Hiddink.

'Sometimes we from the past get a bit too hung up about recognition; I don't. As far I'm concerned, I've got ample recognition over my time in football. But I accept that it's politics. In sport, politics—as in any politics—once your time is up, move on. It's no good sitting around waiting to be recognised. You move on and you allow other people to contribute. People don't talk too much about Keating and Hawke and Fraser any more; they talk about John Howard. Rightly so. And football's the same.'

David Hill, in every way a man who came before his time in Australian football, has similarly moved on. Today he is finishing a book about child migration, bringing up his five-year-old son and pursuing his interest in classical Greek archaeology. With no agendas to push, no backs to scratch, no backroom stoushes to fight, he's blissfully content with his lot—and happy to apportion credit for the game's renaissance to the FFA.

'What this mob has got that I didn't have, they're not accountable to all those old vested interests,' he said. 'The FFA are accountable to no one. This is absolutely remarkable in Australian corporate history. They can make decisions in the interests of soccer, whereas every earlier administration made decisions to cater to the interests of the incumbent vested interests. I don't think the FFA has put a foot wrong. Of the big three things they've done, qualifying for the World Cup I regard as the least of all the achievements; the two really big ones are the A-League, which has been a phenomenal success, and getting into Asia. Lowy must take the credit for that.'

Ironic, too, given that as one of the original architects of old soccer, he's now running new football. Lowy can permit himself a chuckle: 'Life changes. You are young and then you become old, that's all.'

On the biggest day in Australian football history, the *Sydney Morning Herald* ran a double-page story inside its morning edition under the triumphal words 'BIRTH OF A FOOTBALL NATION—AND THE FANS HAVE THEIR EYES ON THE PRIZE'. Underneath, photos showed Socceroos and *Azzurri* supporters having the time of their lives on the streets of Kaiserslautern. Later that day, just as Fabio Grosso would fatefully elude Mark Bresciano, so the tantalising dream of an improbable World Cup progression would slip from our grasp. Amid the grief, emotion, anger and depression that followed, something important was missed. That Australians had the belief, no matter how momentary, that their team could not just beat Italy but could go on to win the world's biggest sporting tournament meant the headline was wrong. Australia hadn't come out of nowhere. Those 15 days in June didn't make us a football nation. We already were. We just couldn't see it.

EPILOGUE

'I don't go through life cursing the fact I didn't win a World Cup. I played in a fantastic team that gave millions of people watching a great time. That's what football is all about ... there is no medal better than being acclaimed for your style.'

JOHAN CRUYFF IN *BRILLIANT ORANGE*
BY DAVID WINNER (2000)

Australia might have some way to go before we play football as stylish as the great *Oranje* teams of the 1970s, but with Guus Hiddink's legacy and Robert Baan preparing to make his own imprint on our national teams, we have begun the journey. What we already have in reasonable measure is integrity. As Mark Viduka said, Aussies are 'fair and honourable', our country is 'perfect, with no agendas'. In this new century of globalised football, such qualities are rare and it is to our country's credit that the Socceroos aspire to uphold them whenever and wherever they play. With a few historic exceptions, traditional 'sportsmanship' still has a place in our national football team, unlike in our national cricket team, where sledging is second nature and defeat is rarely taken well.

This is something that is its own medal. But there will come a day soon when the Socceroos' goodness, fighting spirit, stamina and grit will not be enough if we want to win a World Cup. Frank Lowy, in his determination to nab a world-class coach, has arrived at that point already. Any perceived loss for our national identity in putting a foreigner in charge of our national team has been more than compensated by what we stand to gain in its place: experience.

Australian football is at a crossroads. We have a choice: do we want to remain plucky battlers who, on their day, shock the world? Or do we want to become elegant but wily artisans whose place in the top echelon of FIFA rankings is a given? As Johnny Warren argued, we have to move on from being satisfied with qualifying for a World Cup to actually being able to win it. The conviction we can do it is there—Germany 2006 showed us that—but the necessary foundations—cultural, technical, developmental, financial—have yet to be set.

The 2006/'07 European club season proved just how much we still have to do to get to that next level. With the notable exceptions of Mark Viduka, who produced some of the best football of his life for Middlesbrough, and Jason Culina, who got a taste of Champions League football for PSV Eindhoven, it wasn't the best year for our Aussies abroad. Of the 23 players selected for Australia's campaign at Germany 2006, only two (Mark Bresciano to Palermo and Luke Wilkshire to FC Twente) moved on to bigger clubs in Europe. Just one of the home-based players (Michael Beauchamp to FC Nürnberg in Germany) negotiated a move overseas. The highest profile transfer involving an Australian was Lucas Neill's controversial move from Blackburn Rovers to relegation-threatened West Ham in the January window—controversial because he turned down a competing offer from Liverpool. Neill opted for London, he said, because he 'felt wanted' by the Hammers and, though he maintained money was no issue, was pocketing two or three times the pay. In his first game for his new club, Neill walked off with ankle ligament damage on 50 minutes; in his comeback match a fortnight later he lasted just half an hour before pulling up again. The only positive to emerge in the whole sorry saga for Neill was a get-out clause in his contract that allowed him to leave the club if the Hammers took the drop.

Some of Neill's team-mates from Germany fared even worse in their post-World Cup careers. Liverpool's Harry Kewell and

Nürnberg's Josh Kennedy sat out their respective seasons with long-term injuries, Kewell undergoing multiple operations on his groin and left foot and Kennedy suffering the embarrassment of rupturing an Achilles tendon in his first training session. Then, when he looked like he could return to the field after eight months on the sideline, Kennedy went under the knife again to have a cyst removed from the same ankle. Tim Cahill and Craig Moore were also dealt long spells of inactivity due to injury.

Three players who missed out on match action in Germany, however, made loud statements in their club careers. For so long on the outer in the Premiership, Wigan's Josip Skoko hustled his way into the starting XI in November and didn't look back. Back-up defender Beauchamp scored his first Bundesliga goal in February 2007. Archie Thompson made headlines around the world when he scored five goals for Melbourne Victory in front of 55,000 people in the 2007 A-League grand final. Such is the beautiful capriciousness of football. No player, no team, can ever get too big for their boots. Also-rans become heroes. Stars become chumps.

At this crucial stage of Australia's growth as a football nation, we are no closer to finding a way to stem the drain of our best players overseas—over 150 are known to be with clubs abroad—but these considerable losses are for the first time being balanced by the return of old hands with a lot still left to give. The fact that recent Socceroos such as Ljubo Milicevic, Danny Tiatto and Paul Agostino have all decided to return to play in the A-League is an encouraging sign of the sport's health. The skills and experience they've gained internationally will elevate the local game and help improve standards.

Having Australian teams in the Asian Champions League should also make our best young talent think twice about heading to Europe. In March 2007, Sydney FC and Adelaide United took on China's top two club sides in their respective debuts and were far from outclassed—Sydney brilliantly beating Shanghai

Shenhua United in Shanghai and Adelaide losing at home to Shandong Luneng courtesy of an unlucky own-goal. But with Australian football on show to hundreds of millions of viewers, and a restrictive salary cap still in place in the A-League, our administrators need to be mindful that a whole new front could open in their fight to keep quality players at home. When Ryan Griffiths opted to leave Rapid Bucharest on a loan deal in March for Chinese Super League team Liaoning FC—a middling outfit based in the grim city of Fushun near the North Korean border—the salary on offer was still many times what he could make in his home country. In the global marketplace, no league is too foreign, no frontier too far, as long as the money is right.

The faces of the players graduating from suburban footy fields to the A-League are the most stirring aspect of this new chapter in our football story. At the World Cup, the Socceroos showed the world not only that they could play differently, but also that they came from a very different Australia. While we still produce 'new Harry Kewells' such as Nathan Burns and Kristian Sarkies, a strong young generation of indigenous talent is emerging—Jade North, Travis Dodd and David Williams—and players of African (Bruce Djite, Tando Velaphi, Nikolai Topor-Stanley), Asian (Kaz Patafta) and South American (Alex Brosque, Nick Carle) origin are lining up to be considered the Socceroos' stars of tomorrow. In our national football team, as happened in France in the 1990s, we are beginning to see just how rich and diverse our society really is.

The World Cup will come to Australia, of that there can be no doubt, but it may take another 32 years or more to get here. The lack of suitable stadia across the required number of host cities is not an insurmountable problem, but it will require judicious planning and a huge injection of capital to mount an effective bid. It's early days yet, but with David Beckham blazing a trail in American Major League Soccer, the United States is an early favourite for 2018, with England or Spain likely to snare the hosting rights for 2022. But anything is possible. When John O'Neill turned out for the cameras in early 2007 as consultant for a new NSW Government major events taskforce, snaring the World Cup was first and foremost in his plans.

His old employer, the FFA, was turning its attention to two less ambitious but similarly important projects. As this book was going to press, Ted Smith, the 1956 Olympian and convener of the Socceroo Club, told me he hoped to formally launch the club, with the governing body's official imprimatur, at functions prior to the Uruguay and Argentina matches in June 2007. Meanwhile, Archie Blue was organising an April reunion of his 1965 teammates. Forty-one years, five months and four days since they staggered off Phnom Penh's Stade Olympique in their last World Cup qualifier, Tiko Jelisavcic's men were finally being honoured with their own numbered caps.

In late March, in its last pre-Asian Cup hit-out before meeting its old South American foes in June, the Socceroos played a warm-up international against China in Guangzhou, winning comfortably 2-0. Australia was making up for lost time in its new confederation. From 1967 to 1986 the Socceroos had played twice as many games against Asian national or club sides as it had between 1987 and the start of the 2007 Asian Cup.

But the game was also notable for another reason: the recall of Nick Carle after three years in representative purgatory. His stellar form in the A-League had become impossible to ignore, even for Graham Arnold, once a firm non-believer.

The Australia coach's tune was changing on other fronts, too. Where before he had been adamant about his need to win the Asian Cup come hell or high water, Arnold now spoke of the need to 'build depth ... as we look ahead to the 2010 World Cup qualifying campaign'. They were positive if belated words to hear from someone who said he 'wasn't looking backwards anymore'.

I was preparing to make my own trip in July. I didn't need a palm frond to paddle through the Straits of Malacca to get to Bangkok, just a cheap plane ticket and a credit card. But even more than my Germany trip the year before, the possibilities were intriguing: depending on how the Socceroos performed, I could expect to visit up to four Asian countries: Thailand, Vietnam, Malaysia and Indonesia. Just by having Australia at the Asian Cup, I was about to learn so many things I never expected to know, eat things I would never dare to at home and encounter rodents for which no encyclopaedia had a name. Football matches might last just 90 minutes, but the experiences they leave you with last a lifetime.

I went to my local bookshop to browse the shelves for books about Thailand and turned up a copy of *The Beach* and a pulp thriller called *Bangkok 8*. I'd once been trapped in Bangkok airport for four days (on my honeymoon, no less), and it wasn't a memory I was particularly fond of. But I was willing to give Thailand another try. Just like me, thousands of other fans were dusting off their replica jerseys, booking annual leave and getting ready to follow the Socceroos across the world all over again—perhaps even make a few Thai friends in the process.

Only the chickens were getting nervous.

THE FIRST 500 SOCCEROOS

1922

1. Alex Gibb
2. George Cartwright
3. Dave Cumberford
4. Jock Cumberford
5. William Dane
6. Peter Doyle
7. Alan Fisher
8. Bill Maunder
9. C. Shenton
10. Tom Thompson
11. Dave Ward
12. J. Bratten
13. George Brown

1923

14. Mosie Burton
15. Cliff Gedge
16. Percy Lennard
17. James Love
18. W. Mitchell
19. Sid Robinson
20. J. White
21. Jack Gilmour
22. Johnny Peebles
23. Rob Austin
24. Judy Masters
25. Ernie Owen
26. Gilbert Storey

1924

27. Toddy Edwards
28. Frank Gallen
29. Andy Henderson
30. Frank Millier-Smith
31. Eric Nunn
32. Tommy Oliver
33. H. Sherringham
34. Stan Bourke
35. William Faulkner
36. Jim Robinson
37. Harry Spurway
38. Charlie Leabeater
39. Roy McNaughton
40. Henry Maunder
41. G. Rowe
42. Cecil Williams
43. G. Bristow
44. John Orr
45. G. Raitt
46. F. Ramsey
47. Arch Lambert

1933

48. Alec Cameron
49. Roy Crowhurst
50. Jim Donaldson
51. Jack Evans
52. H. Gorring
53. Jimmy McNabb
54. Bert Murray
55. Charlie O'Connor
56. Jock Parkes
57. George Smith
58. Ian Davidson

59. Jack Hughes
60. F. Smith
61. Tom Tennant
62. Bill Edwards
63. F. Laidlaw
64. James Osborne
65. J. Taylor

1936

66. Ray Bryant
67. Alec Forrest
68. Jim Harden
69. Billy Price
70. Vic Sharp
71. Jim Wilkinson

1938

72. Bill Coolahan
73. Alf Henwood
74. Alf Quill
75. Max Wynn
76. C. Brittain
77. Lex Gibb
78. Fat Kitching
79. Tom Parry
80. E. Petie
81. Harold Whitelaw
82. Aub Mascord
83. Ian Evans
84. A. Mackey
85. Frank McIver
86. Bill Morgan
87. A. Roth
88. Alf White

1947

89. Norman Conquest
90. Dave Coote
91. Jim Cunningham
92. Reg Date
93. Ted Drain
94. Cec Drummond
95. Alec Heaney
96. Ray Marshall
97. Joe Marston
98. Charlie Stewart
99. Ron Hughes
100. Bill Wilson
101. Dick Kemp
102. Robert Murray

1948

103. Jock Hodge
104. Ken Hough
105. Allan Johns
106. Bob Lawrie
107. Frank Parsons
108. Angus Drennan
109. Alan Duncan
110. Gordon Nunn

1950

111. Eric Hulme
112. Tom Jack
113. Kevin O'Neill
114. Harry Robertson
115. George Sanders
116. Jack Smith
117. Bob Young
118. Cyrill Nichols

1954

119. Ron Adair
120. David Bone
121. Lou Hearne
122. Jack Mather
123. Harry Rice
124. Frank Sands
125. Les Suchanek
126. Malcolm Wild
127. Bob Bignall
128. Bill Henderson
129. Jack Lennard
130. Cliff Sander
131. Bill Murphy

1955

132. Clem Higgins
133. Colin Kitching
134. Frank Loughran
135. Cliff Almond
136. Ken Learmonth
137. Ralph Piercy
138. Sid Thomas
139. John McCarthy
140. Albert DePaoli
141. Bill Mahoney
142. Con Purser
143. Ron Burns
144. Ron Lord
145. Mildo Mueller
146. Phil Peters
147. Doug Wendt
148. Alan Garside
149. Bill Paddocks
150. John Pettigrew

151. Ken Vairy
152. Alwyn Warren

1956

153. George Arthur
154. Graham McMillan
155. Bruce Morrow
156. Ted Smith
157. Pete Stone
158. Brian Vogler

1958

159. Jim McCabe
160. Harry Murdoch
161. Lou Vella
162. Bob Wemyss
163. Norm Rule

1965

164. Stan Ackerley
165. John Anderson
166. Archie Blue
167. Pat Hughes
168. Billy Rice
169. John Roberts
170. Les Scheinflug
171. Nigel Shepherd
172. Geoffrey Sleight
173. Dave Todd
174. John Watkiss
175. Roy Blitz
176. Billy Cook
177. Steve Herczeg
178. Jim Pearson
179. Billy Rorke

180. Ron Giles
181. Ian Johnston
182. Hammy McMeechan
183. Johnny Warren

1967

184. Ray Baartz
185. Peter Fuzes
186. Alan Marnoch
187. George Nuttall
188. Alan Westwater
189. John Giacometti
190. Cliff van Blerk
191. Atti Abonyi
192. George Keith
193. Tommy McColl
194. Frank Micic
195. Roger Romanowicz
196. Dick van Alphen
197. Billy Vojtek
198. Manfred Schaefer
199. Ray Richards
200. Ron Corry
201. Gary Wilkins
202. Ted de Lyster
203. Ray Lloyd

1968

204. Ross Kelly

1969

205. Adrian Alston
206. Danny Walsh
207. John Perin
208. Gary Manuel

209. David Zeman
210. Willie Rutherford

1970

211. George Blues
212. Mike Denton
213. Jim Mackay
214. Jack Reilly
215. John Roche
216. Peter Wilson
217. Dennis Yaager
218. Col Curran
219. John Doyle
220. Sandy Irvine

1971

221. Alan Ainslie
222. George Harris
223. Jimmy Rooney
224. Max Tolson
225. Ernie Campbell
226. Bryan Turner

1972

227 Branko Buljevic
228. Bobby Hogg
229. Jim Armstrong
230. Terry Butler
231. John McDonald
232. Bogdan Nyskohus
233. Doug Utjesenovic

1973

234. Jim Fraser

1974

235. Peter Ollerton
236. David Harding
237. Harry Williams

1975

238. Murray Barnes
239. Col Bennett
240. Todd Clarke
241. René Colusso
242. Mike Micevski
243. Agenor Muniz
244. Duncan Cummings
245. Gary Byrne
246. Ray Ilott
247. John Nyskohus
248. Rudolfo Gnavi
249. Jim Tansey
250. John Russell
251. Alan Maher

1976

252. Mark Jankovics
253. Richard Bell
254. John Davies
255. Kevin Mullen
256. Phil O'Connor
257. Mendo Ristovski
258. Peter Stone
259. John Kosmina
260. Gary Marocchi

1977

261. Peter Sharne
262. David Jones

1978

263. Gary Cole
264. Kris Kalifatidis
265. Peter Laumets
266. Josip Picioane
267. John Stevenson
268. George Christopoulos
269. Steve Kokoska
270. Sebastian Giampaolo
271. Sauro Iozzelli
272. John O'Shea
273. Steve Perry
274. Joe Senkalski
275. John Karaspyros
276. Gary Meier

1979

277. Paul Degney
278. Tony Henderson
279. Eddie Krncevic
280. Steve O'Connor
281. Joe Watson
282. Greg Woodhouse
283. Arno Bertogna
284. Ken Boden
285. Tommy Cumming
286. Ivo Prskalo
287. Martyn Crook
288. John Coyne

1980

289. Peter Boyle
290. Jim Campbell
291. John Yzendoorn
292. Alan Davidson

293. Yakka Banovic
294. Vic Bozanic
295. Steve Hogg
296. Paul Kay
297. Danny Moulis
298. Ian Hunter
299. Mark Brusasco
300. Jim Muir
301. Theo Selemidis
302. Jamie Paton
303. John Spanos

1981

304. Steve Blair
305. Bill Rogers
306. Peter Katholos
307. David Mitchell
308. Robert Wheatley
309. Alan Niven
310. Glenn Ahearn
311. Oscar Crino
312. Mark Koussas
313. Grant Lee
314. Jim Patikas
315. Peter Raskopoulos
316. Brett Woods
318. Howard Tredinnick

1982

319. David Ratcliffe
320. Charlie Egan

1983

321. Marshall Soper
322. Jim Cant

323. Terry Greedy
324. Graham Jennings
325. Charlie Yankos
326. Ken Murphy
327. Peter Tredinnick

1984

328. Wally Savor
329. Frank Farina
330. Ian Gray

1985

331. Zarko Odzakov
332. Robbie Dunn
333. Jeff Olver
334. Graham Arnold
335. Tom McCulloch

1986

336. Ange Postecoglou
337. Paul Wade
338. Chris Kalantzis
339. Steve Maxwell
340. Garry McDowall
341. Sergio Melta
342. Alan Hunter
343. Andrew Zinni

1987

344. Charlie Villani
345. Rod Brown
346. Scott Ollerenshaw
347. Jean-Paul de Marigny

1988

348. Mike Petersen
349. Mike Gibson
350. Andrew Koczka
351. Alex Tobin
352. Vlado Bozinovski
353. Robbie Slater
354. Gary van Egmond
355. Warren Spink
356. Joe Palatsides
357. Jason Polak
358. Paul Trimboli
359. George Haniotis

1989

360. Steve Calderan

1990

361. Andrew Bernal
362. Mehmet Durakovic
363. Tony Spyridakos
364. Kimon Taliadoros
365. Ernie Tapai
366. Robert Zabica
367. Jason van Blerk
368. Tony Krslovic
369. Branko Milosevic
370. Robert Hooker

1991

371. Alistair Edwards
372. Milan Ivanovic
373. Aurelio Vidmar
374. David Lowe
375. Ned Zelic

376. Tony Vidmar
377. Paul Okon
378. Greg Brown
379. Andrew Callanan
380. Andrew Marth
381. Aytek Gene
382. Milan Blagojevic

1992

383. John Filan
384. Darren Stewart
385. Mike Grbevski
386. Zeljko Kalac
387. Abbas Saad
388. Tony Franken
389. Mark Talajic
390. Damian Mori
391. Carl Veart
392. Gary Hasler

1993

393. Steve Corica
394. Stan Lazaridis
395. Mark Bosnich
396. Dominic Longo
397. Mark Schwarzer
398. Francis Awaritefe
399. Matthew Bingley
400. George Slifkas

1994

401. John Markovski
402. Mark Viduka
403. Steve Horvat
404. Ross Aloisi

405. Gabriel Mendez
406. Kevin Muscat

1995

407. Tony Popovic
408. Danny Tiatto
409. Craig Moore
410. Joe Spiteri
411. Frank Juric
412. Sean Cranney
413. Jason Petkovic

1996

414. Goran Lozanovski
415. Harry Kewell
416. George Kulcsar
417. Walter Ardone
418. Paul Agostino
419. Craig Foster
420. Kris Trajanovski
421. Lucas Neill
422. Lorenz Kindtner
423. Robert Enes

1997

424. Mark Babic
425. David Zdrilic
426. Luke Casserly
427. Robert Trajkovski
428. John Aloisi
429. Josip Skoko

1998

430. Paul Bilokapic
431. Fausto de Amicis

432. Troy Halpin
433. Brett Emerton
434. Nick Rizzo
435. Alvin Ceccoli
436. Simon Colosimo
437. Brad Maloney
438. Kasey Wehrman
439. Scott Chipperfield
440. Glenn Gwynne
441. Hayden Foxe
442. Raphael Bove

2000

443. Shaun Murphy
444. Stephen Laybutt
445. Pablo Cardozo
446. Matthew Horsley
447. Clayton Zane
448. Richard Johnson
449. Clint Bolton
450. Michael Curcija
451. Stuart Lovell
452. Con Blatsis
453. Mile Sterjovski
454. Jacob Burns

2001

455. Michael Petkovic
456. Archie Thompson
457. Scott Miller
458. Angelo Costanzo
459. Lindsay Wilson
460. Con Boutsianis
461. Mark Bresciano
462. Mark Robertson

463. Sasho Petrovski

2002

464. Patrick Kisnorbo
465. Ante Milicic
466. Jade North
467. Tom Pondeljak
468. Bobby Despotovski
469. Robert Middleby
470. Dean Anastasiadis
471. Ante Juric
472. Joel Porter

2003

473. Vince Grella

2004

474. Ahmad Elrich
475. Nick Carle
476. Tim Cahill
477. Max Vieri
478. Adrian Madaschi
479. Alex Brosque
480. David Tarka
481. Luke Wilkshire
482. Jon McKain

2005

483. Jason Culina
484. Ljubo Milicevic
485. Michael Thwaite
486. Joel Griffiths

2006

487. Michael Beauchamp

488. Ante Covic
489. Scott McDonald
490. Brett Holman
491. David Carney
492. Josh Kennedy
493. Neil Kilkenny
494. Mark Milligan
495. Kristian Sarkies
496. Travis Dodd
497. Michael Valkanis
498. Matthew McKay
499. Ryan Griffiths

2007

500. Shane Steffanuto

Courtesy of Andy Howe/Football Federation Australia

ABBREVIATIONS

AAP Australian Associated Press
ABC Australian Broadcasting Corporation
AFC Asian Football Confederation
AFL Australian Football League
AIS Australian Institute of Sport
ARU Australian Rugby Union
ASEAN Association of Southeast Asian Nations
ASF Australian Soccer Federation (now defunct)
ESPN Entertainment and Sports Programming Network
EU European Union
FFA Football Federation Australia
FFF Fédération Française de Football
FIFA Fédération Internationale de Football Association
JFA Japan Football Association
MCG Melbourne Cricket Ground
NRL National Rugby League
NSL National Soccer League (now defunct)
NTC National Training Centre
OFC Oceania Football Confederation
PFA Australian Professional Footballers' Association
RCS Racing Club de Strasbourg
SBS Special Broadcasting Service
SCG Sydney Cricket Ground
SS *Schutzstaffel* (Protective Squadron, Nazi secret service)
UEFA Union of European Football Associations
VFL Victorian Football League (later AFL)

ACKNOWLEDGMENTS

I owe a note of gratitude to the following cast of characters who offered me their friendship, advice, wisdom, time, encouragement and practical support during the writing of *15 Days in June.*

IN GERMANY AND FRANCE Rod and Tegan Morrison, Neil Jameson, Keith Harris, Sam Pilger, Cameron Fink, Matthew Hall, Anita Bulan, Santo Cilauro, André Krüger, Ted Smith, Toby Forage, Mike Butler, Karl Schutt, Sarah Morton, Aline Arzrouni, Svante Hadell, Kerstin Avemo, all the Socceroos who gave their time generously in the 'mixed zone'.

IN ENGLAND Andrew Jennings, Mark Viduka, Lucas Neill, Basil Scarsella, Kate Pollard.

IN AUSTRALIA Emma Schwarcz, Megan Taylor, Simon Davis, Pauline Haas, Craig Foster, Graham Arnold, Rale Rasic, Jill Margo, Frank Lowy, George Negus, Simon Hill, Les Scheinflug, Robin Graham, Sir Arthur George, Ian Brusasco, John Constantine, Phillip Wolanski, John Boultbee, David Hill, Paul Wade, Paul Lederer, Greg Stock, Richard Kreider, Andy Howe, Kyle Patterson, Bonita Mersiades, Caroline Strachan, David Flaskas, Samantha Bleuel, Ken Lambert, Luke Benedictus, Alléric Mitchell, Daniel Feiler, Thang Luong, Gerald Gallagher, Robin Darnley, Karen Soo, Peter Smith, Adam Mark, Ray Baartz, Stan Ackerley, Archie Blue, Billy Rorke, Billy Cook, John Watkiss, Hammy McMeechan, John Roberts, Jim Shrimpton, Manfred Schaefer, Atti Abonyi, Dennis Boland, Les Murray, Nicki Tsourekis, Patricia Villanueva, Mark Ryan, Edmond Parilo, Gavin Freeman, Andy Harper, Steve Horvat, Carl Hammerschmidt, Vanessa Radnidge, Chuck Smeeton, Andy Withers,

Cornell van der Heyden, Paul Hansford, Jeff Wells, Ben Waterfall, Connie Cenfi and all the girls at Belli Bar, my parents Jan, Fred, Carol, Frank (RIP) and Rosie.

IN HONG KONG Tara Bennett.

IN SOUTH KOREA Pim Verbeek, Afshin Ghotbi, John Duerden.

IN CAMBODIA Charles McDermid, Scott O'Donell.

IN JAPAN Fred Varcoe, Steve Barme, Futoshi Nagamatsu, Ivica Osim.

IN ITALY Mark Bresciano.

IN SPAIN John Aloisi.

IN MALAYSIA Mohamed bin Hammam and Clare Kenny Tipton.

BIBLIOGRAPHY

Crawshaw, Steve, *Easier Fatherland: Germany and the Twenty-first Century*, Continuum, London, 2004.

Elon, Amos, *Journey Through a Haunted Land: The New Germany*, Holt, Rinehart & Winston, New York, 1967.

FitzGerald, Stephen, *Is Australia an Asian Country?*, Allen & Unwin, Sydney, 1996.

Grant, Sid, *Jack Pollard's Soccer Records*, Jack Pollard Pty Ltd, Sydney, 1974.

Hall, Matthew, *The Away Game: The Secret Lives of Australia's Soccer Superstars*, HarperCollins, Sydney, 2000; rev. ed. Hardie Grant Books, Melbourne, 2006.

Harper, Andy, *Mr and Mrs Soccer*, Random House, Sydney, 2004.

Hiddink, Guus & Van den Nieuwenhof, Frans, *Dit is Mijn Wereld*, Tirion Sport, Baarn, 2006.

Jennings, Andrew, *Foul! The Secret World of FIFA: Bribes, Vote Rigging and Ticket Scandals*, HarperCollins, London, 2006.

Margo, Jill, *Frank Lowy: Pushing the Limits*, HarperCollins, Sydney, 2000.

Moffett, Sebastian, *Japanese Rules: Why the Japanese Needed Football and How They Got It*, Yellow Jersey Press, London, 2002.

Murray, Les, *By the Balls: Memoir of a Football Tragic,* Random House, Sydney, 2006.

Olivier-Scerri, Gino, *Encyclopaedia of Australian Soccer 1922-88,* Showcase Publications, Sydney, 1988.

Schwarzer, Mark, *Mark Schwarzer's World Cup Destiny: From Sydney to Stuttgart,* ABC Books, Sydney, 2006.

Solly, Ross, *Shoot Out: The Passion and the Politics of Soccer's Fight for Survival in Australia,* Jacaranda Wiley, Milton, 2004.

Warren, Johnny & Dettre, Andrew, *Soccer in Australia,* Paul Hamlyn, Sydney, 1974.

Warren, Johnny & Harper, Andy & Whittington, Josh, *Sheilas, Wogs & Poofters: An Incomplete Biography of Johnny Warren and Soccer in Australia,* Random House, Sydney, 2002.

Weiland, Matt & Wilsey, Sean (eds), *The Thinking Fan's Guide to the World Cup,* Abacus, London, 2006.

Winner, David, *Brilliant Orange: The Neurotic Genius of Dutch Football,* Bloomsbury, London, 2000.

WEBSITES/BLOGS

Asian Football Business Review: footballdynamicsasia.blogspot.com (now defunct)

The Atlantic Magazine: theatlantic.com

The Beautiful Game (Roger Cohen): blogs.iht.com/tribtalk/sports/worldcupcohen (now defunct)

Brazzil Magazine: brazzil.com

Center for Strategic and International Studies: csis.org

Football (Japan) Lost in Translation: footballjapan.blogl4.fc2.com (now defunct)

Foreign Policy Magazine: foreignpolicy.com

Fox Sports Australia: blogs.foxsports.com.au/football (now defunct)

The Global Game: theglobalgame.com (now defunct)

Jadran Sport: jadransport.org (now defunct)

Information Builders: informationbuilders.co.uk/ontheball (now defunct)

Institute for War & Peace Reporting: iwpr.net

OzFootball Webzine: ozfootball.net

Play the Game: playthegame.org

Racing Club de Strasbourg: rcstrasbourgalsace.fr (official); racingstub.com (unofficial)

Soilent Green 1969: brilliantomiya.blogspot.com

The Southern Cross (André Krüger): ak-tsc.de

JOURNALS/RESEARCH PAPERS

Milanovic, Branko, 'Globalisation and Goals: Does Soccer Show the Way?', *Review of International Political Economy,* Vol. 12, No. 5, December 2005.

ABOUT THE AUTHOR

Jesse Fink was born in London in 1973. He is the author of five books, including the international bestsellers *Bon: The Last Highway* (2017) and *The Youngs: The Brothers Who Built AC/DC* (2013). His most recent book is *Pure Narco* (2020), the life story of former cocaine trafficker Luis Navia.

COPYRIGHT

First published iin 2007 by Hardie Grant Books

This edition published in 2021 by Ligature Pty Limited
34 Campbell St · Balmain NSW 2041 · Australia
www.ligatu.re · mail@ligatu.re

e-book ISBN: 9781922730190

ligature *un*tapped

This print edition published in collaboration with Brio Books, an imprint of Booktopia Group Ltd

Level 6, 1A Homebush Bay Drive · Rhodes NSW 2138 · Australia

Print ISBN: 9781761281440

briobooks.com.au

The paper in this book is FSC® certified. FSC® promotes environmentally responsible, socially beneficial and economically viable management of the world's forests.